GETTING TOGETHER

GETTING TOGETHER

by Eric Weber
and
Sharon Rudman Williams

Edited
by
Allan Ishac

SYMPHONY PRESS, INC.
TENAFLY, NEW JERSEY

Copyright © 1977 by Symphony Press, Inc.
Revised Edition: 1982 by Symphony Press, Inc.
Typeset by Patricia Lee Filip, Input Incorporated
All rights reserved under International and Pan-American Copyright Conventions.
Published in the United States by Symphony Press, Inc., Tenafly, New Jersey 07670
Manufactured in the United States of America.

0-914094-04-1 ISBN

GETTING TOGETHER

Starting today, you can meet and date dozens of attractive, interesting new people.

Starting today, you can begin a deep, loving relationship that will last as long as you want it to.

Starting today, you can rediscover the joy of having someone "special" back in your life.

by Eric Weber
and
Sharon Rudman Williams

Edited by Allan Ishac

GETTING TOGETHER

Table of Contents

HOW TO FEEL REALLY GOOD ABOUT
    YOURSELF 13

HOW TO MASTER THE ART OF BEING
    OUTGOING 19

BREAK RIGID PATTERNS OF BEHAVIOR
    AND ACT IN A POSITIVE WAY 23

WHY YOU DON'T HAVE TO LOVE
    YOURSELF 27

WHY YOU MAY BE DRESSING DULL 31

SMILE AND THE WORLD SMILES
    WITH YOU 35

CULTIVATE FRIENDS OF THE SAME
    SEX 39

HOW TO GET OVER YOUR SHYNESS AND
    BEGIN SAYING AND DOING THOSE
    THINGS YOU'VE ALWAYS
    WANTED TO 43

AN EASY-TO-LEARN SYSTEM FOR
   INSTANTLY TRIPLING YOUR SELF-
   CONFIDENCE WHEN YOU MEET
   NEW PEOPLE 47

WHY SPREADING YOURSELF THIN IS
   A GREAT IDEA 53

HOW TO MEET NEW PEOPLE EVEN IF
   YOU'RE BOGGED DOWN IN A
   RELATIONSHIP THAT'S GOING
   NOWHERE 59

USING YOUR INNER DIALOGUE TO
   LOOSEN UP ANYWHERE. 63

HOW TO ATTRACT PEOPLE WHO AT
   FIRST SEEM COLD TO YOUR
   ADVANCES 67

HOW TO TELL IF SOMEONE LIKES YOU 73

HOW TO MAKE SOMEONE YOU LIKE
   FEEL SPECIAL WHEN THEY'RE
   WITH YOU 79

FIFTY NICE THINGS TO DO FOR HIM
   AND FOR HER 83

A SIMPLE, UPFRONT WAY OF LETTING
   SOMEONE KNOW YOU'RE ATTRACTED
   TO THEM, WITHOUT SEEMING
   DESPERATE 91

ELEVEN VERY ORIGINAL, MOSTLY
   INEXPENSIVE, FUN DATES TO
   IMPRESS SOMEONE SPECIAL 95

HOW TO BRING OUT THE WITTY,
   CHARMING SIDE OF YOUR PER-
   SONALITY WHEN YOU FEEL YOUR-
   SELF STARTING TO CLAM UP 103

FORCE YOURSELF TO GO OUT
   (AND 75 MORE WAYS
   TO MEET NEW PEOPLE) 107

HOLD A PARTY AND MEET
   NEW PEOPLE 117

A SIMPLE WAY TO TRICK
   YOURSELF INTO BEING LOOSER
   AT PARTIES 127

MEET SCORES OF FASCINATING
   NEW PEOPLE IN PLACES YOU'D
   LEAST EXPECT 131

KEEP SOMEONE INFATUATED WITH
   YOU DATE AFTER DATE
   AFTER DATE 135

TWENTY-FIVE WAYS TO IMPROVE
   YOUR APPEARANCE 139

HOW AND WHY YOU SHOULD GET
   REALLY PERSONAL WITH
   THE PEOPLE YOU MEET 145

LEARN HOW TO PROJECT A HEALTHY,
   NATURAL SEX APPEAL 153

How to feel really good about yourself

If you think of yourself as unattractive and dull, that's exactly how others will see you. Once you discover your true potential, learn to think of yourself as attractive, fascinating, sexy—you'll be delighted at how success after success comes your way. You'll look better, you'll feel better—and because you're self-confident, people will be drawn to you like a magnet.

When you look in the mirror each morning, what do you see there? Do you greet yourself with "Hi, gorgeous!" Or with "Ugh—you again?" Unfortunately, most of us have negative feelings about ourselves—about the way we look, our conversation, our taste in clothes, wit, charm.... How many times have you walked down the street, seen someone attractive, and thought, "Why don't I look like that?" or "Why can't I dress as stylishly as that?" How often have you heard someone make a remark at a social gathering and said to yourself, "Now why didn't I think of that?" This is the "if only" syndrome—"if only" we were better-looking / sexier / wittier / smarter / richer / taller / shorter / younger / older / more aggressive / better dressed ... the list of "if onlys" is endless.

It's a vicious cycle. The more you succumb to the

"if only" syndrome, the less chance you give yourself to realize your *own* potential, to become the attractive, interesting person that you *can* be — that you really *are*.

It's a well-known fact that <u>self-confidence breeds success,</u> and success in turn breeds more success. It's equally well-known that mind has a tremendous influence over matter — that when you sincerely believe yourself to be enticing, attractive, intelligent, irresistible, you will communicate that message to others by the way you look at them, the way you move, smile, speak — everything about you will convey the message eloquently to the opposite sex.

Take the case of a young woman we'll call Mary Ann. When she was in high school she tried out for a part in a play — the part of a young, sexy nurse. She didn't get the part, and she overheard the drama coach telling someone that she wasn't sexy enough. Now, Mary Ann wasn't at all bad-looking. She had nice features, wavy ash blond hair, a good figure. But she was shy, inhibited, dressed conservatively, wore her hair in a short, plain style, never flirted. She was terribly afraid — of being rejected, of being thought "cheap." She told herself she wanted people to respect her, to admire her intellect. Well, they respected her, all right — and she never got asked for a date. She spent more lonely Friday and Saturday nights than she cares to remember. She took the coach's words to heart, and more than ever, thought of herself as plain, dull — not the sexy type. Not the type that appealed to men.

When she started college, it became clear to her during orientation week that college life was going to be very different from life in high school. She thought it would be only right to change herself a little too. After all, none of these people had known her—she was starting fresh. She decided to experiment slightly. She let her hair grow long and wore it loose. She bought some clothes that were a little more striking, a little more revealing—body-hugging sweaters in shades that flattered her blond coloring, close-fitting slacks. She bought eye makeup to make her pale eyebrows and eyelashes a bit darker. Before she went to her first class in her "new look," she checked herself in the mirror—and was startled. "Is that *me*?" she thought. "Why, that girl's actually ... *sexy*!" She liked it, but it scared her a little too to see that attractive stranger in the mirror.

It didn't scare anybody else, though. On the contrary. As she walked to class, Mary Ann drew appreciative glances from boys—and male professors. One good-looking young man in her class stared at her during the whole hour. And when the class was over, he asked her if she'd like to get a cup of coffee.

It was the closest thing to a date Mary Ann had ever had. She had always been terrified of boys, but he actually seemed shy, almost as if he were afraid of *her*! They talked for an hour. He seemed to want to say something but was having trouble getting it out. Finally he managed to blurt out, "Are you doing anything tonight?"

Mary Ann couldn't believe it. This tall, well-dressed nice-looking guy was actually asking her for a date! She said she was free, and they arranged to do their class assignments together, and then go to the Freshman Mixer. "You know," he confessed, "I was kind of afraid to ask you. I mean I thought you'd surely have a date already. You being so pretty and all...."

When Mary Ann got back to her room that night,

her cheeks were pink and her eyes glowing softly. She had danced every dance, and she had two dates for the following weekend. Life in college certainly **was** going to be different!

Needless to add, Mary Ann didn't spend any lonely weekend evenings that year. She **knew** she was an attractive woman, and her walk, the things she did with her body, her facial expressions, gestures, tones of voice — all these gave the message, loud and clear, to the world. Men responded to her; and the more they responded, the more her self-confidence increased.

There are all too many people who never discover themselves as Mary Ann did, who never manage to liberate themselves from the cycle of **feeling** dull, plain and unappealing leading to **being** dull, plain and unappealing, in turn leading to feeling even duller and plainer and so on. But you **can** break the cycle; you **can** free yourself from the trap that is preventing you from being the magnetic person you are meant to be.

Take another good look in the mirror. Everyone has some good features — what are yours? Play them up; dramatize them. Do you have blue eyes? Buy a shirt or sweater of a deep, rich blue and see how it brings out your eye color. You can do the same thing with brown or green or hazel eyes. Go to a good hair stylist and get the cut and style that's really right for you. Do you have an attractive body? Make the most of it with clothes that really show it off to advantage, even if they cost a little more than you usually spend. If you can afford only one outfit to start with, make it a really smashing one — the investment will pay off. If your body leaves something to be desired, embark on a determined exercise program until you whittle it into shape. If you're a woman, study the art of applying make-up. Then watch people's eyes when they look at you. Did you know the pupils widen when people see something pleasant? The first time you see that happen will be a great ego-booster — and it *will* happen.

Now what about your conversation? Do you often feel at a loss for words in a social gathering? Spend as much free time as you can becoming really well-informed about what's going on in the world. Read newspapers, magazines, watch information shows on t.v. Go to see a couple of those new movies that everybody's been talking about. Then accept every invitation you receive and throw some parties yourself. Invite new people; tell your friends to bring their friends. You will now have the ammunition to talk, so use it! Learn to listen well too; state your views with quiet conviction or with passion, whatever you feel; but don't be afraid.... You'll find it's far easier than you thought.

Watch the reactions of the opposite sex when you walk down the street, enter a restaurant or a nightclub. They'll look at you with approval, once *you* really believe you are worth looking at. Don't say to yourself, He — or she — *can't* be looking at me! He or she *is*, and they like what they see. If you like what you see, too, go ahead and look right back — plenty of terrific relationships have gotten started in just that way: with an approving glance.

How to master the art of being outgoing

Look for eye contact. Be vigilant, be watchful. Look! People are always looking to see if someone is looking back. Be a looker and a watcher. Then be a talker and a listener and an answerer-back. And you're on your way. You're on your way to mastering the art of being outgoing.

A friend of mine who is a cold-weather freak tells me how he turns even that peculiar aspect of his personality to advantage on the streets of New York City. He says, "I walk crosstown every morning and every evening to get to and from work, and in the winter I really enjoy the walk on especially cold days. Now, most people don't, and they just bundle up against the wind, squint their teary eyes and look down and try to get wherever they're going as fast as possible. Such people I just ignore as I pass them by. But what I do is look for the ones who, like me, are enjoying the cold weather, and with them I try to make some contact. I look for the ones who are smiling at the sudden icy blast of wind that's blown up Sixth Avenue, or the one who's just caught a snowflake on her tongue and is tasting it and looking for another one. With these people I exchange smiles and simple expressions of oneness of mind. As with everything else, it's so much nicer to be able to share the experience with others. And the obvious pleasure is infectious. A like-minded soul will not hesitate to return the offering. When we stop for street lights we say things like, 'Great day, huh?' or 'Isn't New York great on a day like this?' The response is always a good one.

Another friend tells me how he simply looks at everyone he passes, no matter where, and never averts his eyes. It's a system that works so often that when you do it all the time the number of successful contacts you make is phenomenal. I recall being on a short ferry boat ride with him once, returning from Fire Island, and watching the way he behaved. Simply by looking at people and being ready with something to say, no matter how trite (usually it was nothing more extraordinary than 'Hi. How are you doing?') which would lead into a conversation. By the time that thirty-minute trip was over, he (and I, through him) knew about half the people on the boat.

That's the first part of the job—being open and ready and willing to look like you're open and ready and willing to engage in small talk, a conversation, a relationship. Look like someone who is in the habit of talking to people and carrying on relationships with them at all levels, from the most casual to the most intimate. By which I mean that once the original eye contact has been successfully made, be ready to follow it up with a conversational gambit. Many people often think that the art of making small talk is to appear not to be making small talk at all. If that's your style, fine. But that need not be the way it is at all. On the contrary, you can be very directly and openly "making small talk"—saying things like "That's a marvelous ring," or

"Where did you get that T-shirt?" or "Great beard you've got"—rather than "Who do you think you'll vote for?" or "What do you think of Lina Wertmuller's latest film?" These latter can be follow-up lines of conversation, as can many other classic ones. But for starters, you can say something as obvious as "Do you think the rain will hurt the rhubarb?"—and in fact, something obvious may be the most effective thing you can say.

Part of looking like you want to be part of what's going on, part of being outgoing, is looking the part. This means that off-putting facial and verbal expressions won't do, nor will body posture that says, "leave me alone." No frowns or furrowed brows, no nervous fingers and scrunched shoulders. An open mouth showing teeth, smiling, laughing easily, merry eyes, hands and arms that wave and gesture a lot, a head that turns readily, arms that welcome and accept rather than exclude and reject. Be careful that the message of the face and body is genuinely reflecting what you feel, if what you feel is positive and part of the outgoing attitude you're developing. There is nothing quite so dismaying as to find that the message being conveyed by your body is very different from the one that you thought you were conveying and were trying to convey. Everything has to be in turn with everything else.

Finally, after you've made the initial eye contact, after you've followed up by developing a direct and open conversation, there remains the problem of being physically outgoing, of being unafraid to use your body. This is often the most difficult of all things for the habitually shy person to do. Getting up in front of people and moving often requires the largest dose of nerve. But it must be done. When there's music, that's all that most people do anyway, and if you do it with self-confidence and ease it will look like you've been doing it all your life and never given it a second thought. And just to move in general — around a room, from person to person, from group to group, when circulating among people, when leaving a restaurant, entering a room, going to the john, all this is being physical, and doing it with confidence, ease, some grace and total relaxation, so that it looks like you've always been in the habit of just moving. And being willing to move as well as actually moving instills confidence. One feels so much better walking around comfortably, knowing that people see you but aren't **watching** you, and knowing that you're walking around and not sitting in some corner wishing that you didn't have to go to the john so that you wouldn't have to run such a long gauntlet to get there. Just do it, unselfconsciously, naturally, simply, and try talking to some people on the way and making eye contact, and otherwise showing how much you've mastered the art of being outgoing.

You'll be amazed at how much this kind of thing then elicits the desired reaction. Being outgoing engenders a climate in which it is easy to become even more outgoing, because people are reacting to this warm, accepting, involved, exciting, adventurous, relaxed, natural and enjoyable person.

Break rigid patterns of behavior and act in a positive way

Do you sometimes feel as if you'll never be able to change the way you behave, even though you know perfectly well that your behavior is self-destructive? All of us feel that way at certain times. We find ourselves repeating patterns of behavior that we've noted before and condemned in ourselves as stupid and totally counterproductive. Yet here we are doing those same stupid things again. Why? And *can* you change your behavior? The answer is a resounding *Yes.*

Of course, it's a question of habit. It's not easy to change overnight a lifetime of behavior patterns. It takes time, effort, determination, hard work, concentration and devotion. You have to be a missionary to yourself, devoted to the cause of changing and keeping changed all those behavior patterns that you've identified as self-destructive. Constant vigilance is the watchword here: A kind of vigilance that, we hope, becomes second nature after a while — but nonetheless a real vigilance against any backsliding, any repetition of the bad old ways.

First of all, whenever you are going to be with people in a social setting, do whatever is necessary to get yourself into a good frame of mind. Keep in mind that if you go into a social situation feeling negative you're going to chance having a bad experience, and thereby reinforce negative feelings about yourself and your ability to change. Whether it means having a warm, relaxing bath, or doing exercises, or meditating, or taking a nap—whatever makes you feel good, refreshed, happy with yourself and the world—make sure you do it beforehand.

Putting yourself into a positive frame of mind is the first item on your checklist—for the whole crusade, and each time you're going to be in a situation where your bad habits might reassert themselves. But once you are off and running, be sure to keep the vigilance high. Be aware of how you're feeling and what kind of signals you're sending out. If your problem is withdrawing, clamming up, do you find yourself sitting in a tightly curled-up position like a cocoon? Have you not said anything to anybody for the past twenty minutes? If you see symptoms that you recognize, admit it to yourself; and decide right then and there what you're going to do about it. Have another drink. Get up and go over to a group. Begin to talk about something that interests you. It's possible to do that in a nice way by saying, "Excuse me for changing the subject, but there's something I'd really like to talk about." Or ask someone to dance. Or just go and get something to eat, or visit the men's or ladies' room. Do whatever will give you the impetus to collect yourself and your thoughts and put them back on the track of the "new" you.

This kind of vigilance can be difficult and tiring, which is why it's imperative to work very hard at it when you begin. Once the new habits have begun to replace the old, you can begin to relax a little. The whole process of watching out for danger signals will then have become almost second nature.

About a year ago I was introduced to an attractive woman named Germaine, with soft brown hair and big, expressive blue eyes. I expected her personality to match her appearance, and was quite surprised to realize that in almost every conversation she would become hard, judgmental, righteously indignant. Eventually I decided to mention it to her and see if she was aware of it herself — it was a habit that certainly wasn't going to do her any good.

She bit her lips when I brought it up. "Yes, I know I do that," she said. "Everything will be going along fine, I'll be enjoying myself and making a good impression on everyone else — and then all of a sudden I'll feel this need to form a judgment about somebody I'm with or somebody we're talking about. It's as if I'm trying to establish my credentials, to show that I'm not just anybody, that I can make fine distinctions, draw conclusions about people. I don't know, it's as though if I didn't do that I'd be letting myself down, failing to live up to my own high standards."

We had a long conversation. I tried to make Germaine see that she wanted people to think of her as the high priestess of taste, culture, morals, and everything else. Why couldn't it be enough for her just to be pleasant company, to know how to enjoy herself and to be sensitive to other people? "Stop preaching," I said. "Turn it off. Preachers are bores at parties and poor company for dinner. They belong in pulpits or on soap boxes." Was she planning to become a minister or a politician? If not, she'd have to stop judging people. Or she'd find herself being judged — as the least wanted person around.

Though Germaine had been conscious of her bad habits, I made her see how offensive they really were and how destructive they could be to all her opportunities in life. I talked to her again a couple of months later. "That did it," she said. "I made a decision that I was going to change. I began listening to myself, really listening, and at the first hint of preachiness I changed the subject. Or just shut up. I always made an effort to be good company, to think about what other people felt and needed rather than what I thought of them. It worked. And works. And what's best is I rarely have to think about it anymore."

Whether your self-destructive behavior patterns are of the "too much" or the "too little" variety— whether you say too much of the wrong kind of thing or else clam up when you ought to be opening up—vigilance pays off. You're *not* stuck with bad habits, doomed to repeat them forever. You're not on a treadmill. You *can* change, break the pattern and replace it with a new and satisfying one. It's up to you.

Why you don't have to love yourself

It seems that no matter which way we turn, self-improvement books, talk show personalities and magazine articles all tell us that we must love ourselves before someone else can. I disagree. I believe that even if you don't love yourself, you can still meet people, hug people, and love people. And they'll love you back. Let me explain.

Perhaps it's your looks you're unhappy with. Maybe you're a woman with bright red hair and what seems like hundreds of freckles all over your face. In your opinion, perhaps, brown hair is sexier. Therefore a simple equation forms in your mind. You do not have dark hair so you are not pretty. If you don't think you're pretty, you can't love yourself. And no one else can either. But maybe, just maybe, that attractive bachelor a few doors down the hall (the one who always smiles so warmly in the elevator) thinks red hair is dynamite? The fact that *you* don't like your looks, doesn't mean a darn thing to him. He doesn't know that you don't like your looks. And he doesn't know that you don't love yourself. (I'll never tell). So loving yourself, or more correctly, **not** loving yourself, is irrelevant when it comes to getting together with new people.

Sure it would be nice if you loved yourself . . . maybe even great, you think. You might look forward to going out more on weekends, and it might give you the confidence to ask for a raise. But so what? Would loving yourself really matter once you were out to dinner, snuggled close to that attractive bachelor. I doubt it. So, the next time you decide to approach someone for a date (or accept one), remember that there's nothing obvious about you, no glaring neon signs, that tell others you don't love yourself.

If you're still unconvinced, just think of someone you know who you'd imagine loved him or herself. How do you know this . . . after all we just got done saying that it's hard to tell? Well, consider someone who's always struck you as being extremely conceited. How may conceited people do you know with lots of friends? Believe me, very few people are drawn to a person who is infatuated with himself. You're much better off being human and attainable than overconfident and untouchable!

Try discussing what you think of as "your problem" with some of your close friends. I'm sure you'll find that they too feel the same way. You may not realize it, but very few people really love themselves. The ones who do are few and far between.

Take the case of Eloise, an intelligent social worker who serves as an advisor to a large senior citizen group. For a number of reasons, mostly just bad luck, Eloise had a tough time keeping a relationship together. Time and time again, she would fall for the wrong guy and find herself feeling rejected and alone. Although she felt good about bringing happiness into the lives of old people, she just didn't feel good about herself and her own life.

One night, Eloise was feeling particularly low, but decided to go out anyway. Upon arriving at a local lounge she headed for a far corner and kind of slid into the background, where she thought no one would notice her. "I don't even know why I came out," she said to herself. "Who could possibly like me anyway. I don't even like myself."

But someone was watching Eloise and did like what he saw. For he, too, was in that far corner and, in fact, was even more hidden than she. Eloise was so caught up in her own thoughts that she literally jumped when Matthew approached her with a friendly "hi" and a big smile. "What are you doing way back here anyway?" she asked suspiciously. "I guess I'm just trying to stay out of the spotlight." he replied.

With the ice broken, Matthew and Eloise began to talk and he explained that he was feeling particularly down himself because he had just been passed over for a promotion that day. He admitted to Eloise that he had been using the same corner because he felt that no one would want to talk to someone who was feeling so glum.

Although hesitant at first, Eloise responded to Matthew's openness and confessed some of her own feelings about herself. She couldn't believe that a guy as cute as Matthew didn't like himself either. She ended up having a fantastic time in spite of her "problem," and made a date to see Matthew the following weekend. Three months later they were engaged, and neither could care less about loving themselves . . . they were wildly in love with **each other**, and that's all that mattered.

You are the only one that can convince **you** that it's okay not to love yourself. When it comes right down to it, it's very likely that the qualities you find fault with in yourself, are not even noticable to your friends and the people you meet. So, even when you're feeling low, pick yourself up and find someone else to love!

Why you may be dressing dull

There's a desire among many people to disappear into the woodwork, not to be seen, not to attract attention, to be as inconspicuous as possible. On the other hand, many people would like to attract a decent amount of attention, but they don't know how to go about it. In both cases, the way in which the desired — or undesired — end is accomplished is by means of dress.

A basic principle here is the attitude taken toward the human body in general and to one's own body in particular. What do you think and feel about your body? Is it something quite repulsive in your mind? Do you find most bodies repulsive — except for those very few which prove the point by being outrageously gorgeous? Let me tell you something. The difference between extremely beautiful bodies and just average, ordinary nice ones — like yours and mine — is not nearly as great as the difference between the two extremes, the gorgeous ones and the awful ones. CHANCES ARE EXCELLENT THAT YOUR BODY — once you've acquired the proper attitude toward it — is capable of looking every bit as good as most (in fact better than many).

The human body, unless it has been allowed to go entirely to pot, is generally quite a beautiful thing, in both its masculine and feminine forms. If you've taken the initial steps of whipping it into shape through diet and exercise, there's no need to hide or disguise it. A small or medium-sized or generous bosom are three different kinds of attractive bosom, all of which can be taken advantage of in the way one dresses. Wide hips are thought by many men to be attractive, as is an ample bottom; others prefer narrow-hipped women. A small bottom on men appeals to a lot of women, while there are plenty who don't object to a bit more. In short, there is no one acceptable standard of attractiveness. Learn to like and dramatize *your* particular type. Play up your best physical features; but don't try to hide. Baggy pants, for instance, on either a man or a woman, are not likely to show off the advantages of one's bottom half, and besides that they are inherently, unattractively—baggy.

If you're dressing dull, you may very well have some hangups about the body in general and about your own in particular. Search out friends whose manner and style of dress appeal to you. Find out how they feel about bodies, about themselves and about clothes and dressing. If you are not able to get adequate answers that way, don't be hesitant about seeking professional help. Go to the makeup and fashion departments and consultants of good stores and invest some time and money in the kind of advice that they have to offer there.

If you've accepted a dull image of yourself, you may not find it necessary to look for deep, psychological sources of the problem. You may simply not have very good taste or a sense of style. Whatever the explanation, the result is the same—and the solution can be the same: find out what the best store around is and accept the advice of their fashion consultant. Study fashion magazines: learn how to put outfits together, what colors and patterns and textures look right together, how to use accessories.

Two friends of mine, Jim and Julie, had the same problem: they both had very dull images of themselves. In fact, Jim was asked on more than one occasion after he'd left the seminary why he continued to dress like a seminarian—something that had simply never occurred to him. It had just seemed to be the way to dress—in basic black with black accessories and a rare touch of white. Julie's appearance was not quite so severe, but the end result was pretty much the same—dullsville. Jim changed his style on his own, simply by having been jolted into recognition of what he was doing with his appearance, by hearing enough people tell him the same thing. He dumped his dark clothes and dull image and from then on, each time he shopped for clothes, he did so with an eye to color and cut. Before too long, his image had changed; his own feelings about himself and the way people reacted to him changed.

Julie's problem required more work: "I was aware of the problem, but had no idea what to do about it. Then a friend suggested I go to the fashion consultant at Bloomingdale's. I did. And the results were fantastic. I was shown how pants should fit without being ridiculously and uncomfortably tight. How simple, wrap-around skirts can be very chic and sexy. How a shoe with a low heel can be as smart as and more comfortable and attractive than a spike heel or platform shoe. The most important thing of all, I think, was the insights I got into the use of color. It was made clear to me by showing me examples on models that colors can be used boldly. I was shown a bright, shiny green dress on a black model and it looked smashing. Then the consultant went even further and added a bright orange sash and it looked still more smashing. Of course, I was tempted to tell myself that it looked so good on her because she was so smashing herself, but the point had been made: color could be used boldly, even outrageously, and yet be very attractive. I was shown a layered look incorporating various tones of purple — you know, deep purple vest over violet blouse with mauve skirt and a bright purple belt, and I realized that colors don't have to match, whatever that means. The end result was that it became clear that dressing *boldly* does not mean wearing blouses open to the waist or skin tight pants — though there's nothing wrong with that either, if that's how you want to dress on occasion — but rather that you can be bold and individual simply by putting things together in your own way. Now I always read the fashion magazines, and while I don't copy the outfits there, I get a good idea of how to put together my own. Let me tell you, it's all gone a long way to changing my ideas about a lot of things, about myself and my image and the way people see and relate to me."

So whether it's a deep psychological feeling about the human body or a simple question of poor taste and inadequate sense of style, it can be solved by trying to come to grips with it yourself and/or taking it to a professional for help. It is one of the easiest problems to deal with. It doesn't require a lot of time and money. You have to have clothes anyway. So now you'll just be buying clothes with a better cut, more style and more interesting color. You won't be buying more clothes or more expensive clothes, you'll just be buying different clothes — for a different (and better) you.

Smile and the world smiles with you ...it's true!

Have you ever noticed how some people always seem to be smiling? If you're like me, you've probably wondered what makes these people so damned happy. Have they just won $100,000 in a lottery, closed the deal of a lifetime, moved in with a magazine centerfold?

Probably not. They've just learned that a good old smile for no reason at all can produce some wonderful results. A smile, more so than anything else we can do, is an instant, easy, quick (and inexpensive) way to communicate that you feel good about someone. It can say I think you're special . . . let's get to know each other . . . I'm really attracted to you . . . I'd love to meet you . . . or simply, you look nice.

Try an experiment. The next time you're at a party, a club, or anywhere else you spot an exquisite stranger you'd love to meet, position yourself at an angle that allows the two of you to see each other clearly. Don't worry about what you'll say, because all you're going to do at first is smile.

Turn on the most attractive, dynamic smile you can, and flash it each time the stranger glances your way. The result? In most cases, one of two things. The person you've set your sights on will either walk over to you, having been attracted by your friendliness, or will be waiting anxiously for you to approach them. It's difficult, if not impossible, to ignore a smile and the person that's delivering it. In fact, it's the best ice-breaking method I know.

Examine your smile. No kidding. Stand in front of a mirror and smile. Does your smile look friendly and warm or more like a sinister grin? Are your teeth shiny and white? That's important, too. Work on it if you think there's room for improvement. Keep practicing in front of the mirror until you're pleased with the results. See a dentist if necessary. It's never too late to put on a new smile.

Practice your smile. We all know that practice makes perfect, so get busy. Smile at the people who pass you on the street, the girl at the checkout counter in the supermarket, and the guy who pumps gas at the neighborhood Exxon station.

Use your eyes as well as your mouth. A smile without eye-to-eye contact is like a peanut butter sandwich without the jelly . . . passable, but not great. Try gazing into a person's eyes as you smile at them. It will make your advance much more personal. In addition, it will help the recipient of your smile be **sure** that it is he or she you're smiling at. (Although you never know where a misinterpreted smile can get you!)

I know a very nice, but incredibly shy guy named Harold who would spend most of his evenings on a bar stool staring at the two or three blondes in the place he wished he could meet. While he was a very charming and interesting guy once he got started, his problem was approaching women. "I'd sure love to talk to that girl over there with the light blue turtleneck," he sighed one night. "Her eyes are just gorgeous." "Well, go ahead, she's all alone," I prodded. "That's easy for you to say," he answered, "but once I get off this stool, my legs turn to jelly. I just don't know what to do."

Later that night, after I had watched Harold suffer silently for about two hours, I asked him if he would mind some friendly advice. I told him that I knew of a way he might be able to meet a girl without walking over to her at first (his numero uno fear, you recall). What did I suggest? Nothing more than a good old smile. I told Harold to really turn it on, and at the same time to gaze into the pair of eyes he found so beautiful.

After rearranging his chair for a better view, Harold started to smile, and smile, and smile some more. To Harold's surprise and delight, the girl in the light blue turtleneck began smiling back! A half-hour and a lot of smiles later, Harold turned to me and said "What do I do now? I still feel a bit shaky." But there was no need for me to reply, because lo and behold, the blue-eyed blonde was making her way through the crowd directly toward Harold! Well, Harold took it from there and the story had a very happy ending. The moral? Smile and the world smiles with you!

Cultivate friends of the same sex

Having seen the title of this chapter, you might be saying to yourself, "What do I need more friends of the same sex for? It's the *opposite* sex I want to cultivate. *Vive la difference!*" I'm 100% in favor of *la difference*. But I would like to show you how making more and better same-sex friends can be a rich source of opposite-sex ones — and can, as a bonus, provide you with deep emotional satisfactions.

Women generally have closer friendships with other women than men do with other men — society is more accepting of closeness between women than of closeness between men. Little girls and teen-age girls always have a bosom buddy with whom they exchange misinformation about the "facts of life" and rhapsodize about the boys they have crushes on and agonize over whether they should accept the invitation to the dance from Bill or turn it down and hope for one from Pete and risk not going at all. And grown women usually have one or two really close friends whom they can tell everything to — secrets about their emotional lives that men are trained to keep locked inside themselves.

If you're a man, do yourself a favor: try to find at least one male friend with whom you can really let it all hang out. Men *need* someone to talk to — really talk, not about sports and politics and business, but about personal things, feelings, relationships—just as much as women do. Even when you are involved in a close relationship with someone of the opposite sex—let's face it, you can never be *quite* as open and honest as you can with another man (or another woman). **La difference** is exciting and fascinating and wonderful and none of us would want it otherwise; but it *is* also—different. Someone of the other sex can never—because of that inborn difference—identify with you the way a same-sex friend can.

A word of caution: be absolutely sure your close same-sex friend is someone in whom you can have complete faith and trust. Betrayals have been known to occur.

Okay. Having a close friend of your own sex can be great for your emotional life. But it can be great for your social life as well. Your men friends have sisters, female cousins, women co-workers at their jobs (provided they're not interested in said co-workers themselves), even ex-girlfriends. Men friends can be very understanding and more than willing to fix you up with "this great girl that I know."

On the other hand, women who have close women friends get to meet male cousins, ex-boyfriends, colleagues, "my sister's ex-husband." Married women have husbands who have lots of male friends, colleagues, etc. (Naturally, the same goes for the wives of married men friends, if you're a man.) Same-sex friends have boyfriends and girlfriends who have friends, and who will probably be willing to arrange double dates, or simply provide you with introductions. Same-sex friends have activities that you may be able to get in on: join your friend at his/her evening class or club meeting or on an excursion to the zoo or the museum or the theater or a party where extra guests will be welcome. Of course, you won't want to go *everywhere* with a friend; but sometimes we need a little moral support — especially if we're new at the game of actively looking for opposite-sex contacts — and it can be very comforting to have an understanding friend with you, encouraging you to be outgoing and bold and confident. (Just make sure that the friend won't mind going home alone, if you should connect with someone.)

And of course, your same-sex friend is bound to prove worth his/her weight in solid gold bullion when you're going through a slow period socially. Or if your girlfriend/boyfriend has just bounced you. I wouldn't like to count the number of times I've called up my friend Joe, who works only a few blocks away from where I do, asked him if he was free for lunch, and bent the poor guy's ear for an hour over a hamburger and a double martini, while I complained about the sudden disappearance of attractive and available women from the face of the earth, or my inability to get through one more day of life without the particular woman who had just shown me the door. And the equally astronomical number of times long-suffering Joe managed patiently to point out to me that I would not only survive, I would prevail, and as a matter of fact a new woman had just been hired in his place who was nice-looking and fun and as far as he knew unattached.

Are you convinced that cultivating one or two good friends of your own sex can be one of the best things you ever did for yourself? If not, try it ... you'll like it.

How to get over your shyness and begin saying and doing those things you've always wanted to

Have you ever noticed how the people who flout convention, who do what they feel like doing and say what they think without worrying too much about how people are going to react, are the ones who always get attention? Instead of envying people who say and do the things we'd all like to if we weren't such chickens, say and do them yourself! Don't be afraid to do the unexpected, to be a little bit outrageous.

Of course, you have to be careful to keep clearly in view at all times the dividing line — and sometimes it can be a thin one — between the acceptable and the unacceptably "outrageous." Don't ever be outrageous in a negative, hurtful, insensitive or cruel way. But being careful to avoid these obvious pitfalls, you still have plenty of room in which to be excitingly, astonishingly, zanily "outrageous."

Go ahead, try it. Say or do just about anything that occurs to you. Do a minimal amount of censoring. Then let it flow. It won't be hard to avoid being negative if the mood you've put yourself into before you set out is a positive one—if you can manage to purge yourself of negative feelings and thoughts, you won't even have to pay any conscious attention to censoring. Feel good about yourself, about what you're doing and what you're planning to do. ***Expect*** to have a marvelous time. Then just relax and let it happen.

When you first arrive at a party, have a drink. It will help to loosen you up and overcome your inhibitions. Then, if you see someone who catches your fancy, walk right up to that person and say so. "You know, you're the best-looking guy here!" or "You are a very attractive woman!" Try it once, as a favor to me. I'd be willing to bet that the response will be encouraging and that it'll be easier to do the next time. Of course, no one can guarantee that such an opening gambit will *lead* to anything—the remaining moves have to be worked out. But it *can* be guaranteed that you will get the attention—complete and undivided—of the person you've addressed those words to.

Or try going over to (or sitting down next to) a person who attracts your interest and —in a proper manner, of course—telling them through touch that you are interested. I once met a woman at a party who rewarded the men she found attractive by kissing them on the cheek when she was introduced or introduced herself. It never failed to get at the very least a smile of pleasure.

You might play the devil's advocate—say what you don't believe—in a conversation. Being forced to defend a position you don't really advocate is a marvelous way to overcome shyness. Try disagreeing with a consensus that seems to be developing in a group (you know, where one person says something and all the others sit there and nod their heads in agreement)—just for the shock effect. For example, in a group that is essentially non-religious, announce that you've been born again. Many such "opposite" possibilities present themselves — you can be a prude in a libertine group, a leftist in a conservative group, an ardent proponent of nuclear energy among environmentalists, an advocate of open housing in a nice, homogenous little community, etc. But don't rant and rave and scream it out — be nice. Just quietly maintain your outrageous (to the group you're in) point of view.

A shy friend of mine, Dan, has learned to use his body to assure that he will get attention. He likes yoga and folk dancing, and has found that lots of people at parties are very interested to learn that he dances once a week and does yoga-like and folk dance exercises every day no matter where he is. Since this often leads to requests for more information, Dan has developed the habit of sitting on the floor and demonstrating the series of exercises he generally goes through. "A little group usually gathers around me, in the kitchen or the living room or wherever I happen to flop on the floor, and they stay there entranced for as long as I want to continue it, asking questions, making comments. One part of the exercise is a kind of whoop — a noise that folk dancers often use — and that usually serves to double the size of the crowd gathered around me. They seem not only genuinely interested in what I'm telling them and showing them, but also, by extension, in me. If I can get somebody to ask for this little demonstration early in the evening, it usually makes the rest of the evening for me. It's as simple as that. And a nice bonus is that women often ask if I'd teach them the exercises. I could make a career out of going from house to house conducting exercise classes."

Whether you get people interested in something

you do, like Dan, or do and say things that other people wish they had the courage to — people will admire and respond to you. And by drawing attention to yourself in positive ways, you'll be **forced** to overcome your shyness — after all, you've got to follow your own act, and you won't want to let people down!

An easy-to-learn system for instantly tripling your self-confidence when you meet new people

At the first sign of anyone new on the horizon, most people's self-confidence takes a nose-dive. This is not only counter-productive, it's downright immature. Sometimes the best romances are the result of sheer grit, determination and perseverance.

When you're a tiny baby, all you have to do is say "da-da" and people break into broad grins and cries of delight. Kids are always important and interesting to their little world of family and friends.

Unfortunately, as you grow older, being the center of attention isn't quite so automatic. Adults expect far more of their peers than they do of children. Kids only have to *be*, while adults have to *do* to get recognition. Being attractive, charming and witty is far more of a challenge at twenty-five years of age than at twenty-five months.

What do you do in the face of this challenge? Do you throw up your arms in despair and moan, "Well, I obviously can't *do* anything worthy of recognition, so

I'll just give up right now"? What a life you doom yourself to if you take this way out! The mature person realizes that it can be wonderfully rewarding and fulfilling to grow into the kind of adult that other adults find appealing and interesting. And the mature person understands, also, that this often takes a lot of hard work, practice and courage.

Few of us possess the looks of Robert Redford, the sex appeal of Jacqueline Bisset, the sense of humor of Woody Allen, the intelligence of Henry Kissinger. The vast majority of us are average — in looks, brains and sexiness. In order to rise above that average we have to be willing to get up off our comfortable rumps and make an effort; otherwise we're going to remain "just average" all our lives. Ask any man or woman in love what their lover is like: There can be a million different answers, but it **won't** be, "Oh, she's (or he's) just average." If people are going to like you, love you, want you, admire you, you have to have something that makes you stand out from the crowd. You have to be *special*.

Okay, you say, what do I do to be special? There are thousands of things. And the vast majority of them don't require years of study or huge investments of money or time. What they *do* require is motivation and perseverance. Like it or not, ours is a society that admires people who accomplish things — people who are self-confident because they are special.

I know a young woman named Rickie — an average sort of young woman, 26 years old, who works as a secretary in a legal firm. She's not bad-looking — but no Elizabeth Taylor; she's bright enough — but no Einstein. A couple of years ago, she began feeling very dissatisfied with her life. It didn't seem to be going anywhere. Yet she was frightened of getting into new situations, where she would have to meet new people — she felt she just couldn't measure up. Her activities dwindled to practically zero, and getting up in the morning hardly seemed worth the trouble.

Rickie and I had a long talk. It was clear to me that the root of her problem was that there was nothing *special* about her — nothing that said to the world, "Look at me, I'm worth noticing!" Her repeated failures to attract the people she wanted to attract depressed her, and strengthened her feeling that there was nothing she could do to change.

Once she understood what the difficulty was, I got her to take a good hard look at herself. What were her interests, abilities, things she enjoyed doing — or had once enjoyed and had given up? It turned out that she had loved music when she was in high school, had sung in the choir and taken piano lessons. But it had seemed like "just too much trouble" to pursue that interest later on. She was a good cook, too, although she seldom bothered with gourmet cooking since she almost always ate alone. I convinced her to see what she could make of those interests and abilities. She didn't really want to take up piano again. Well, what about guitar? Yes, that turned her on. Her interest was also piqued by the idea of getting hold of some exotic cookbooks and inviting friends over for dinner.

Rickie bought an inexpensive guitar and started taking once-a-week lessons. She practiced faithfully a half hour every night — folk tunes, popular songs, music people would enjoy hearing and singing at social gatherings. She practiced recipes on her family and close friends, and then invited groups of friends and acquaintances—and people she **wanted** to get to know—to small dinner parties where she cooked the dishes that were most successful. She soon acquired a reputation for being a really fabulous cook. People begged her for her curried chicken and lamb pilaff and Ukrainian borsch recipes, and jumped at the chance to spend an evening at her house. Her circle of friends couldn't help but widen, and naturally, she began receiving return invitations. One evening, when she was going to a friend's for dinner, she casually asked, "Would you like me to bring my guitar?" The friend was startled. "I didn't know you played the guitar! There's no end to your talents, is there?"

Rickie was nervous that first time she played before a group—but her practice paid off. She was no Bob Dylan, but she certainly played well enough for people to enjoy listening and singing along. She became both a more successful hostess and a more desirable guest than she had been before, because she now had something special to offer, and felt happy about it. She found herself meeting far more people—both women and men. She was asked out much more often than she had been before, and, as often as not, by people that she herself considered attractive and interesting. The last time I spoke to her, she told me about a terrific guy she had been seeing for several months.

Of course, Rickie did not become more popular and successful simply because she learned how to play the guitar and brushed up on her cooking skills. Accomplishment has a snowball effect. These initial accomplishments increased her self-confidence and self-esteem and made her feel much better about herself and life in general than she had for a long time. Self-confidence acts like a magnet upon other people because it makes you talk more easily, smile more readily, walk more proudly. In short, it makes you more outgoing and likeable. When you have something you can be proud of, something you *know* is special, people will warm to you. You need never be afraid of meeting anyone new once you acquire that special glow that comes from liking yourself ... and you'll find that friendship, fun and romance will all be far easier to come by than you ever thought possible.

Why spreading yourself thin is a great idea

When people tell you not to spread yourself too thin on the job, heed their warning. When they tell you not to spread yourself thin in love, ignore them. Spreading yourself thin socially is the best way I know of meeting new people and letting others know, "Hey, I've got lots and lots of love to share."

Some people are concerned when they hear this notion: "Are you suggesting I be disloyal to my boyfriend? Paul would be so hurt," or "I've never been out with another woman since I've been seeing Susan. I'd feel so guilty." Look, I'm not suggesting infidelity. If you're married or engaged and feel happy about your love situation, fantastic. There's nothing better than undying love for one person. But I suspect that if you're reading this book, even if you are married or engaged or seeing someone steadily, you're not totally satisfied with what you've got. You want something better, something with a little more excitement, pizzazz, energy. And spreading yourself thin for the next few months might be just the suggestion that can change your love life.

Now, how do you begin to spread yourself thin. First, look around you. Look at your friends. Our society is one of labels. And you can probably label yourself by examining your crowd; preppies, funkies, sophisticates, partiers, etc. Most likely the people you spend the most time with are very similar to you in attitude, lifestyle, background, and personal tastes. It's a natural instinct to be drawn to people most like ourselves, since we feel more comfortable in familiar surroundings.

However, this same instinct to seek familiarity prevents us from broadening our horizons and meeting as many new people as we can. Similar people do similar things, and constant chumming with the same friends limits your experiences.

The first step in spreading yourself thin is to visit places you'd never expect to find yourself. If you're an accountant and you always spend your time with buttoned-up suited companions, sign up for a jazz or aerobic dance class at a local health club. I know, it's not you. But it's okay. This is an experiment that could have spectacular results. If it doesn't work out, your old friends and old haunts are still back there. You'll never know what the "other side" has to offer unless you let your hair down and explore.

If you're not sure where to go or what activity to try first, approach someone in your office or apartment building who you've previously decided is **not** your "type." Ask them where they go to meet new people and invite yourself along or go alone. The more extreme a person you pick, the more drastic and unfamiliar the new event will be, so prepare for the contrast.

Treat your first night out in foreign territory as an adventure. I'm aware that being in a place you've never been before, and feeling like an alien from Alpha Centuri while you're there, can be a little unnerving . . . frightening, too! I won't tell you to relax, because I've always found this suggestion only serves to make you more uptight. But be aware you may feel some unfamiliar sensations, especially if you're alone . . . but nothing longlasting or permanent.

Since you'll be visiting new places you should probably dress for the new scenery. If you usually put on jeans and a V-neck sweater, try something sharp and sexy. Perhaps a smart suit and tie or a clingy black evening dress, or even a total punk outfit. Style your hair differently, dab on extra cologne, unbutton one more button down the front.

After a few dance clubs, cooking courses, or hiking trips (whatever you've chosen as not your usual social menu) you're going to start to meet new people . . . like it or not. Be prepared to accept invitations to do things that may be out of the ordinary for you. You may be used to your crowd finishing up the night over coffee and eggs in the local diner. But should a chic stranger invite you to end the evening at an all night private club, by all means say yes. You just might find that dancing until 5 a.m. beats a hot bagel and cream cheese!

Brian's situation is a good example of "spreading". Since law school at Yale, Brian had been hanging out with the same group of guys. Together they had pulled through dozens of tort law classes and grueling exams and the bond that was created would last forever.

When three of his chums moved to Chicago after graduation, Brian followed (familiarity, of course). Twice each week after work his buddies would meet at the same bar on Michigan Ave., have some beers and shoot the breeze. When they weren't discussing the good old days at Yale, the conversation centered around a tough criminal case Paul was working on, or the controversial judicial decision to desegregate the south end that Fred was involved in.

Six months passed, then a year. The same bar, the same friends, the same conversation. Brian loved his friends but he felt restless. All the lawyers and legal assistants in his firm were men . . . married men with no women friends to introduce to Brian. He felt restless and lonely, and in the back of his mind he knew he was missing something, but tradition was strong and his lifestyle was comfortable, albeit boring.

Then one afternoon in November, Lucy, the only secretary in Brian's office (and dynamite looking,) invited him to a party. Now Brian was a Yale man, and even though he was attracted to Lucy, he couldn't imagine that *her* friends could offer *him* anything. He considered asking her if he could bring his buddies along, but decided this would be in bad taste, and reluctantly accepted her invitation anyway.

When Brian picked up Lucy at her apartment, she was dressed in white tights, a red clingy dress, and she had glitter on the corner of each eye. Immediately his tweed blazer and Bass weejuns began to pale, but he plunged on. A friend of Lucy's who was in advertising had rented a rock club for the night and Lucy said lots of "beautiful people" would be there. "Oh no!" he thought.

When they arrived at the party everyone was dressed like Lucy. Brian felt like a martian. All her friends seemed so wild and crazy . . . so unlike people he was used to spending a Friday evening with. The music was loud and the lights were blinding. But Lucy was a great date. She introduced Brian to everyone, made sure his glass was filled, and taught him to dance a funky dance in a secluded corner (a gesture he appreciated).

Before long Lucy and Brian were center stage. Brian's blazer had come off and he'd unbuttoned his blue cotton oxford to his navel. Oh, this was different alright (if the guys could see him now), but he was having fun! He never once mentioned law and realized what a relief this was. He began to wonder why he had cooped himself up in a quiet tavern for the past year.

From that night on Brian's life was never quite the same. He still met the guys when he could, but he also made a point to try new places and meet new people each week. As time passed, he felt less of an alien when he walked into unfamiliar surroundings and was able to enjoy even the most bizarre experiences. Lucy and he dated every so often—no, she wasn't his type, but she had taught him a lesson in life he couldn't forget. And he loved her for it.

When you get out and explore unfamiliar territory you'll meet all sorts of exciting people, too. You'll date more and always have some event planned for the weekend . . . whether it's a scuba diving lesson in an old quarry, or a lecture on Japanese film. With all these new people in your life you'll also have a chance to share all your feelings and fantasies, all your emotions and loves.

So remember, while it may be a drag to spread yourself thin in life . . . in love, the thinner the better!

How to meet new people even if you're bogged down in a relationship that's going nowhere

A relationship that has turned sour is not a life sentence. Do yourself a favor and get out of the bog before it suffocates you. The world is full of people, interesting people, attractive people — get out there and find them!

Our first responsibility is to ourselves. If you don't like yourself, if you don't take care of yourself, no one else is going to, either. And how can you do anyone else any good if you've let a destructive relationship turn you into a physical or emotional wreck?

One of the first lessons we learn in life is that things and people change. A relationship that starts out beautiful and passionate and completely fulfilling *can* — for any number of reasons — turn into one that is dull and unsatisfying ... or even actually painful. Maybe it was right for you at an earlier stage of your life, but now you've outgrown it. Maybe you've discovered faults in your lover that you didn't know were there in the first hectic, wonderful days ... or simply incompatibilities between the two of you. Whatever the reason, the relationship has soured, like milk that has been left out too long.

But because you committed yourself to it once, are you stuck with it forever? Are you doomed to a wasted life, to lost opportunities, boredom, frustration? Is guilt preventing you from getting out of life what you should be getting — good times, satisfaction, real companionship, someone to share your joys and sorrows with? Are you watching the world pass you by, with all those exciting people that you can never get to know?

This was the way Jed felt. He was miserable with Anne. They just couldn't seem to get along any more. Come to think of it, she didn't seem very happy, either. But every time he thought about leaving her, he was so overwhelmed by guilt, by pity for her, that he couldn't bring himself to make a move, and he hated himself for even thinking of it. Poor girl — how could he leave her alone? How could she manage without him? He thought of her lonely, miserable, crying herself to sleep at night, making the round of singles spots, asking her friends to fix her up ... going to parties and making an effort to meet new people ... being asked out by strange men ... getting back into the whirl ... Hey, wait a minute! That didn't sound so terrible for her, after all. Sure, she would be unhappy — for a little while. But once she started going out again, once she found somebody she cared for, — she would be fine! In fact — and it was a little momentary blow to Jed's ego to realize it — she would be much better off than she was now. He would actually be doing her a favor by breaking off!

What egotists we all are, to think that another person can't survive without us. Once Jed realized that a bad relationship is bad for **both** people involved, he was able to bring theirs to an end without painful guilt feelings. But he didn't want to leave either of them in the lurch. He told Anne he thought they had been seeing too much of each other—and to his surprise, she agreed. They started spending some of their evenings apart. Jed let his friends know that he was available. When he met new people, he was honest—he told them he was in the process of ending a relationship and was getting back into the swing of things generally. He built up his list of new contacts, and he assured himself—through talking to her friends—that Anne was doing the same thing. When he felt that they had had a long enough transition period, and that both of them were ready, Jed took the decisive step. Not long afterward, he heard from mutual friends that Anne was doing just fine. She hadn't spent any time moping, but had gotten out and done things, and as far as anyone could tell, she wasn't a bit depressed. As for Jed, he had a tremendous sense of liberation, of new and wonderful worlds opening to him—and he knew that he had done the right thing for both of them.

No one's pretending that ending a relationship is easy. It is one of the hardest things any of us ever has to do. But life is short, time is precious—why should we be condemned to needless unhappiness?

Nor is it easy to face the prospect of being alone. It's not very pleasant to spend your evenings with the t.v. and the cat when you've gotten used to constant companionship, to having someone you could always rely on. Don't be ashamed of that feeling; it's perfectly natural. No one wants to be lonely. For this reason it's wise, before you break out of your unsatisfactory relationship, to take some steps to ease the transition, as Jed did. Ask that attractive guy in your business management class if he'd care to join you for lunch. Invite the new secretary in the office for a drink after work. Ask your friends to introduce you to their friends.

There's nothing clandestine or sly about all this. You're not trying to trick or cheat anyone. You're just smoothing the way—it's legitimate and it's smart. you don't want to find yourself alone and brooding—and possibly regretting your decision to make the break. If you make plenty of contacts ahead of time, you can ensure a full social life for yourself. And you won't have any regrets—you won't have time!

shoes, and was sure that my date as well as everyone else in the restaurant, must notice my face puckered in pain. I don't know why, but all of a sudden, during an uncomfortable period of silence I blurted out, "I'm really sorry about being so quiet, but my shoes are hurting my feet so much, I can hardly swallow!"

Well, no sooner had the words escaped by mouth, than the two of us went completely wild with laughter. We remained hysterical for about five minutes and everyone in this posh little restaurant looked on in disapproval. What had seemed like an outrageous comment at first had actually worked to my advantage!

Later that night, my date told me that she really admired the openness it took to make the comment I had. In fact, most men and women do admire the quality of frankness in a person, so allow yourself to tap into the thoughts that are whirling through your head, and vocalize them. You're sure to like the results.

A little spontaneity can go a long way in relieving your inner tensions and nervousness. There is nothing worse than ruining a perfectly lovely evening with the pain of a tension headache. But you can avoid it. Since your tension is probably stemming from insecurities which you've built up needlessly anyway, relax and share them with your date! Although you may spend the rest of the evening conversing about your similar neuroses, so what? At least, the silence will be gone and your evening will be filled with laughs.

anything you want, don't you? You don't censor yourself. You don't worry that maybe if you say something a little revealing, a little off-color, a little stupid, that your friends will castigate you and ban you, forever, from being in their company. You act natural, allowing yourself to express the silly parts of your personality that are so much fun for others.

Why not try calling up this "inner you" the next time you're on a date and silence has settled in. Tap your inner dialogue — give voice to the conversations you're having inside yourself that other people rarely hear. You won't sound like a lunatic...you'll sound honest. Even the most annoying questions of self-doubt can be "picked" out of your head and verbalized to your date. Censor nothing.

For instance, you might say something like "you know, I've looked forward to our date tonight all week, and now all I can think about is how shy I'm acting." Sound silly? Not at all. Nine times out of ten, the person sitting across from you is feeling exactly the same discomfort. He or she will laugh nervously, but will feel instantly relieved and more close to you. You've let her off the hook...now she can loosen up and express some of her own inner thoughts. There's nothing like a sharing of feelings to act as a tension breaker.

Have a good laugh at the ridiculousness of these inner thoughts. I can tell you from experience it can change the whole course of a date. One night when I was out with a woman at a trés chic French restaurant, all I could think of was how painful my new shoes were. I just couldn't get my mind off those

Using your inner dialogue to loosen up anywhere

Everyone knows the terror of total silence on a date. You clear your throat, she clears her throat. You shuffle your feet, he shuffles his feet. And the misery grows and grows and grows. It seems the more we want to impress the person we're with, the more charming and funny we want to be, the more difficult it is to relax and find our sense of humor. With same sex friends we're a barrel of laughs. On dates we make Bella Lugosi look like a comedian.

At these times, discouraging thoughts over which we seem to have little control, are shooting through our heads: "Why am I so boring, so withdrawn, so shy?" Sometimes these questions seem so overwhelming we become nervous to the point of panic. We want to run, leaving our date sipping at her bowl of onion soup all by herself.

Here's a little trick you can use that might help during these uncomfortable moments. Think about why you're so much more relaxed, zany and fun-loving when you're with your friends. You say and do

How to attract people who at first seem cold to your advances

You get on a bus (or train or plane) or you walk into a crowded room (or restaurant or theater) — set the scene wherever you like. You see **the** man or **the** woman: the one you really want to get to know, more than you've wanted anything in a long time. You've heard about the importance of eye contact, so you watch, and hope he/she will look back, and you'll have it made. But nothing happens. If he/she does look your way, it's only to quickly glance away again. So you give up. "It wasn't meant to be," you tell yourself.

Or do you?

Are you being fair to yourself, giving up before you give it the old college try? Surely that incredibly attractive man or woman is worth more of an effort than a little staring! Did it ever occur to you that maybe he or she is shy? Doesn't want to believe that you are actually looking at him or her? Is unaggressive? Preoccupied with job worries or a sick relative? Is dying to come over and talk to you but doesn't have the nerve?

I'm going to tell you about just a few of the many,

many ways you can attract someone who doesn't seem interested at first. Do justice to yourself and try some of them, or all of them, before you even begin to think about giving up. But the chances are that they will work so well you won't **ever** have to think of giving up!

Fear of rejection is normal. And we become, of course, even more afraid of being rejected when we don't get an immediate response from the person we're attracted to. But fear is also very counter-productive, because it can paralyze you, defeat you before you begin. And if you let it do this to you, you're handicapping yourself right at the start. You'll never get very far in this life — whether in attracting potential dates and mates or in anything else — unless you have the courage to try and to work.

Along with courage goes confidence. If you walk up to someone so firmly convinvced you're going to be rebuffed and humiliated, you'll probably come on as someone with a poor self-image — and as we've been saying again and again, no one likes a person who doesn't like him or herself.

Okay. You've looked, and the look hasn't been returned. What do you do next? You talk, that's what. And if you're going to bother to talk at all, you might as well take the trouble to say something that will have an effect. It needn't be something profound or brilliant or witty; but it should be something that will make the person take some notice of you — if possible, something that will make him or her think. So **don't** say, "nice day, isn't it?" or "Do you think it's going to rain?" Here are some great opening lines: "You have very interesting cheekbones." "I'll bet you're a Taurus" (or whatever). "Where did you buy those neat glasses?" "How is AT&T doing?" (to someone reading the stock market section in the paper). "Care to dance?" (to someone on a Muzak-equipped elevator with you). "What did they *put* in this drink, anyway?" (to someone standing near you at the punch bowl). "Wasn't I once married to you?" "Don't you think Picasso's blue period was his best?" (to be used in museums). "Do you mind if I put this belt around your waist — you're about the same size as my brother (or sister)" (for department stores). "You must be French (or Italian, Greek, Norwegian, etc.)" "Where have I seen you before?" (oldie but goodie). "That's a great-looking dog. What breed is it?" (To person dog-walking). "Excuse me, but I couldn't help overhearing what you were saying, and I simply had to mention...." "You look bored" (to someone at party who isn't the life of it). "Would you let me share you umbrella?" "Come on in out of the rain." "What did you think of the tenor" (at the opera). "Do you think Baryshnikov's slipping?" (at the ballet). "Please, don't *ever* change that hair style!" "That's the nicest thing anyone's done for me all day" (to someone who's just held a door for you or passed you the sugar). "Is Riesling dry or fruity?" (in a liquor store).

Those are just a few examples — there are thousands more that *you* can think of. If your initial approach elicits some response and leads to a conversation, you can follow up and make sure she/he *knows* for sure you're interested by saying something like "You are without a doubt the best-looking (or most interesting, or most intelligent) man (or woman) here." "I've been following you for blocks. Didn't you notice?" "I've been trying to get your attention for hours." "I certainly hope this won't be the last time I ever get to talk to you."

A friend told me that once, while she was reading at one of the long tables in the New York Public Library, a note was suddenly pushed under her nose. She unfolded it and read: "I'm harmless, just lonely and bored. Would you care to join me for a cup of coffee? If you say no, I'll understand." She looked up to see an attractive young man smiling at her across the table. She just couldn't resist such an honest and ingenuous approach. She smiled back, and that was the beginning of a delightful relationship.

You've looked, you've talked, and you think you may be starting to get some results. What else can you do?

Your body talks even more eloquently than your tongue. If you're sitting on a couch with the Interesting Person, turn your body towards him or her. Chances are he or she will do the same. Two people turned towards each other tend to send out a "keep-away" message to other people.

Smile.

Touch. This is a powerful signal, and to be used with care. You don't want to come on as lecherous or clingy. But a light touch, when appropriate—on the shoulder, or arm, or hand—can be very exciting. Touching yourself can also be stimulating and seductive to another person. Again, not blatantly—casually stroke your thigh, put your hand on your hip, run it through your hair, etc.

Listen. Listen carefully to what the other person is saying. Remember his or her name and use it. Store up the information and use it to ask intelligent questions. Impress him or her by how well you remember what's been said to you.

And persevere! Believe it or not, most people are

probably shyer than you are, less self-confident. Even if someone is looking at them persistently, talking to them, smiling, coming on like gangbusters, they have trouble believing that it's meant for *them*. Many women remember their mothers warning them, as little girls, not to talk to strange men. And plenty of men have grown up believing women are passive creatures who *never* show interest in the opposite sex.

So don't give up at the appearance of coolness or dis-interest. The chances are excellent that it's being used as self-defense, to avoid disappointment or hurt, or, in the case of women, to avoid appearing "easy." If there's *any* response at all—the flicker of an eyelid, a slight smile, a turning toward you, a word or two—keep trying.

Of course, no one is successful *every* time. But even if you should lose out on this one—so what? That wasn't the last attractive man or woman in the world, was it? Next time, you'll succeed!

How to tell if someone likes you

How many times have you started talking with an attractive member of the opposite sex at a party or a dance and thought to yourself: I'll bet she notices my bald spot ... or, I wish I had a more interesting job to talk about...or, if only I had worn something more expensive or stylish-looking.

This is a depressing, destructive, but unfortunately common phenomenon. Many of us automatically assume that anyone we find romantically appealing won't reciprocate. That as attractive and interesting and dazzling as we find them they find us homely, dull, lacklustre....

Come on, admit it. Think of all the times you excused yourself to go for a drink because you were afraid you were "trapping" someone who didn't really want to talk to you? And how many times have you avoided calling someone up for a second date because you were sure they would say no.

Now I want you to ask yourself this. Are you sure you were right? How do you really know you were "trapping" someone? Were they actually squirming or wincing? Did they go so far as to **tell** you that they didn't want you cornering them like this?

And what about all those wonderful people you never called back for a second date? Don't you think you might have been wrong about some of them? Isn't it just possible that two or maybe even half of them actually liked you...or maybe even had a tremendous crush on you...or, if you want to really let your mind roam free, isn't it just possible that some of them were actually downright miserable that you never called them back?

The reason I ask is that it's been my experience that many of us assume we know exactly how other people feel about us when in fact we are just projecting out our own feelings of insecurity and self-effacement onto them. The truth is that we are often dead wrong.

Think of all the times others have misinterpreted the way you felt about something. About whom you were going to vote for, about which team you were rooting for, about what man or woman you thought was attractive, about how much you liked or didn't like a particular person.... The list is endless. People think they know what others are thinking and are as wrong as they are right....

Let me tell you a little story. I have a friend. We'll call him Charlie. In college Charlie had a crush on a girl in his speech class. Judith. Charlie was shy, quiet, introspective, a little on the bohemian side. He wore combat boots, long hair, workshirts, and carried a funky green book bag over his shoulder. Conversely, Judith was a psi phi, one of the cutest, most vivacious sorority girls on campus. Charlie often saw her walking between classes with one of any number of handsome, well-groomed, crisp, clean fraternity boys.

One day Carlie and Judith wound up chatting after

speech class. Charlie had given a speech on Amsterdam, and since Judith was going there that coming summer she wanted to know more about it. They fell into a friendly, enjoyable conversation. Charlie had expected her to be cold, calculating, on guard ... but she turned out to be lively, easy to talk to, uncritical. She relaxed Charlie, made him feel free. Since he was basically a witty, interesting guy, he really began to come to life. He made Judith smile and then giggle and then laugh. Pretty soon she was roaring, and Charlie laughed along, he was so happy and sort of proud to be cracking her up.

But then, right in the midst of all this hilarity, something awful happened. Charlie got hit by a vicious case of the doubts.... Suddenly he felt Judith was just being nice ... or if she really was finding him so funny then maybe as a clown, not as a potential boyfriend. Charlie stiffened up, looked at his watch, and said he'd better go now, that he had to be getting back to his room to study for a big test. Judith stopped laughing. She looked at him a little bit oddly, not really understanding Charlie's sudden withdrawal. Oh, what the hell, she thought to herself, I guess it really must be a big test. She took what he had to say at face value. The two of them left the building, said goodbye sort of formally, and parted company at the next fork on the path across campus.

After that things were never really the same ... Charlie's crush for Judith grew larger every day, and as it did he grew more and more afraid of her, sure that her social life was so rich and luxurious that she really had no interest in him ... that one afternoon of friendly laughter was a freak occasion ... a momentary lapse in her defenses.

The semester ended, Charlie transferred to another university, and that was that. No romance, not even a date, between Charlie and Judith. Despite that wonderful fifteen minutes of spontaneous and pleasurable togetherness. But our story does not end here.

Ten years go by. Charlie and Judith are thirty now. Charlie is a copywriter in an advertising agency, married, the father of a child, a successful and energetic young man on the way up in the world. Judith has become an actress, and a fairly successful one at that. She is divorced—her marriage to a rather conventional fraternity man left her feeling uninspired, unfulfilled, and she ended it just two years after it began....

Now picture this ... It's a radiantly clear Thursday morning in early summer. Charlie is at a casting session with his art director, Paul, and his producer Tom. They are looking for an actress to play the part of a young mother in a tuna fish commercial. A tall redhead finishes reading her lines, says her goodbyes, and walks out, praying quietly to herself that she's landed the part. In walks the next applicant, a lively, vivacious brunette. It is Judith, the girl Charlie had loved from afar during sophomore speech class. She takes one look at Charlie, her face breaks into a broad happy grin, and she runs up to him and hugs him. "Charlie Allen!" she exclaims. "I can't believe it!" she says, turning to Paul and Tom. "You know, I had the maddest crush on this guy in college and he was so stuck up and intellectual he never asked me out." Then she turns back to Charlie and gives him a big kiss.

I needn't tell you how absolutely floored Charlie was. He felt heppy and sad all at the same time ... thrilled that she too had had a crush on him, but an immense sense of loss that he had so woefully misinterpreted her feelings about him. He wondered how many other romances he had missed out on because he had mistakenly assumed the woman he'd been attracted to wasn't at all attracted to him.

Now what about you? How often has this happened to you? And what are you going to do about it?

My advice is simple and direct: <u>Instead of assuming the new people you're meeting aren't attracted to you, assume just the opposite. That they find you good-looking and interesting.</u> And instead of looking for all the little signs that tell you they don't like you, look for the ones that indicate they do like you. What are they? There are millions of them: Did they look you straight in the eye ... smile at you ... use your name when they addressed you ... touch your arm while they talked to you ... asked you questions about your job, where you live, where you're from, where you went to school ... told you about themselves, what they do, what sports they play or hobbies they have.... Did they laugh while chatting with you ... ask how you are ... light your cigarette ... offer you a chair ... sit down next to you ... offer you the dip ... wonder what sign you were born under ... say you look like someone they know ... tell you they had a dream about you ... ask you where you vacationed ... inquire about your health ... ask you what kind of music you like?

The list is endless. But I'll bet the next time you talk to someone new you'll discover them showing you one and possibly quite a few more of the above signs that indicate they like you ... that they want to know you better.

And when they do show you these signs, don't

ignore them, don't overlook them, don't say to yourself, Ah, I must be dreaming. These signs are real, and meaningful, and important ... and they can be the beginning of many a loving and enduring relationship.

How to make someone you like feel special when they're with you

We all like people who like themselves, and we all like people who make *us* feel good about ourselves. It's really not difficult to make a person you like feel that they must be very special indeed ... and they'll like you all the more for it.

You can't project good feelings to other people if you are totally absorbed in yourself. Your very first step is to dump any feelings of self-pity, any grudges you might have against the world, down the drain. From now on you are going to turn outward instead of inward, you are going to look up instead of down, you are going to concentrate on other people instead of yourself all the time. You're going to stop wondering "Am I being foolish?" "How are people reacting to me?" and start thinking "how do *they* feel?" "is he or she having a good time, feeling good?"

Of course, all this isn't totally altruistic. Opening up to other people, concentrating on making them happy, has the very pleasant side effect of making them like us more.

Start with what people see first and look at most of the time — your face. Do you have a habitual frown or a blank stare? That can make people feel that you disapprove of them or are indifferent to them. But if you smile at someone, you convey the message "I like you." "You appeal to me." "Something about you makes me feel good." The act of smiling opens the door for other people to begin to respond to you. In fact, it's very hard *not* to respond to a smile. People you don't know will smile back, maybe stop and talk. Friends will enjoy having you around more than they did before. And the person you are especially interested in will know that you enjoy being in his or her company, and that there must be something pretty super about them to make you feel that way.

Learn people's names. *Use* them. There's nothing worse for someone's ego than to have their name forgotten. When you meet someone who interests you very much, listen carefully to what they say — don't concentrate so intensely on being witty and brilliant yourself that you forget you're involved in a conversation, not a monologue. Remember what they tell you — about their job, their interests, their childhood, or whatever. And when appropriate, let them see that you remember, that all this is important to you. They will be tremendously flattered and will feel that they must be pretty wonderful — and that you are a person of considerable intelligence and good taste to have recognized their sterling qualities.

A little actual flattery never hurts, either. Obviously you don't want to lay it on with a trowel. You don't want to say something that's obviously untrue — if a girl is built like Twiggy, for instance, you don't want to tell her that her body is incredibly voluptuous. But you *can* say that slim, graceful women really turn you on, that whatever she wears she looks marvelous in, etc. If a guy is on the short side and in need of a little muscle-toning exercise, you wouldn't tell him how big and strong he is. Find something you can *genuinely* compliment him on — his sense of humor, his smile, his eyes or hair or artistic hands or intelligence or perceptiveness or how he always knows how to say just the right thing or that you love being with him. He will visibly glow with pleasure and you will rise several notches in his estimation.

And why not come right out and tell someone how special they are, that they're wonderful, that they mean a great deal to you? That's the greatest compliment of all.

People like to be touched. Even someone you've just met will respond (if they're at all attracted to you, and you can judge that pretty well by the way they look at you and talk to you) to a touch — on the hand, the shoulder, the cheek ... just how intimate the touch should be will depend on how far the relationship has progressed and the vibes you're getting. You have to judge that for yourself. But remember that touching shows a desire for closeness, for a deeper relationship; it shows that you're attracted and interested. It's exciting, and it will generally make the person want to respond in kind.

All of these techniques can be summed up in the general concept of getting out of yourself and concentrating on the other person, on what *they* need, what *they* want, what gives *them* pleasure. If you genuinely care, are genuinely interested, it will almost automatically show in the things you do and say. Your very bodily movements will express your interest and admiration — the body doesn't lie. But a little effort, a little thought given to how to please someone you like can only increase the good effect.

Let me give you a quick example of what I'm talking about. I was on a plane once, going from San Francisco to Los Angeles, when a really attractive woman sat down next to me. I liked her at once, not only for her looks, but for the way she apologized, smiling, for taking up so much room under the seats with her packages. It was a short flight, and I knew I'd have to work fast. We got into conversation, and while I knew my evident interest showed in my eyes and my smile and my gestures, I gave it a helping hand by saying, "You know, it's always been a fantasy of mine that one day a beautiful, intelligent, fascinating woman would sit down next to me on a plane. It's finally happened, and I can't quite believeit." She was delighted. Before that hour-long flight was over, I had her phone number in San Francisco, and promised to call her next time I was in town — which I did, and we had some really good times together.

<u>Think about others, think about making them feel good, and you won't have to worry about how you're coming across to them. They can't help but like you.</u>

Fifty nice things to do for him and for her

A lot of people worry that after they meet someone special, and date for awhile, that they won't know how to keep the magic or energy of the relationship alive. My answer to that is always the same. If the chemistry between two people is right, the magic doesn't disappear—it may evolve, it may seem to be stronger some days than others, but it's always there.

I have had people tell me, however, that doing something special for someone, even a little thing like bringing them home-made soup when they're under the weather, can enhance an already good relationship and make it even better. I've accumulated a list of those suggestions, and here they are: Fifty nice things to do for him, and fifty nice things to do for her.

Most involve little preparation and can be done with little money. You can try them after you've been seeing someone for a day, a week, a month or a year... ten years even. The beauty in all of them is simply that they say, "I care". And that can work powerful magic on any relationship!

Fifty nice things to do for him

1. Send him a special card sprayed with his favorite perfume.

2. Drop off a six pack of his favorite beer.

3. Hand him two tickets to a Yankee game (wait for him to invite you to come).

4. Collect his laundry. Wash and iron it for him.

5. Drop off a homemade box lunch at his office.

6. Get him a gift certificate at his favorite athletic store.

7. Serve him a candlelight dinner (dressed very sexy).

8. Embroider his monogram on some of his favorite sweaters.

9. Put together a basket of instant soups, beverages and packaged nuts...for the times when he's too busy to leave his desk.

10. Give him a herbal facial.

11. Invite his family to dinner at your place.

12. Take him on a "mystery ride" to your favorite spot in the whole wide world.

13. Manicure his nails.

14. Make him new curtains for his apartment.

15. Buy him a see-through negligee (in your size).

16. Offer to sew on his missing buttons.

17. Treat him to a course of "massage for couples" (very popular and *not* expensive).

18. Buy him dinner at his favorite restaurant.

19. Take his best friend and him to a baseball or football Hall of Fame.

20. Stock his refrigerator with his favorite foods.

21. Buy him a terrific new cologne.

22. Make him a homemade pizza from scratch.

✓ *23.* Give him a foot-massage (read up if you haven't the slightest idea where to start).

24. Frame a great picture of you and him for his desk or dresser.

✓ *25.* Buy him a "how to" book on something he's expressed interest in learning about.

26. Bake him his favorite cake (write a love note on it).

27. Give him a subscription to a sports magazine.

28. Clean his apartment.

29. Take his car for a wash and wax.

30. Crochet him a tie (or sweater if you're an expert).

31. Give him a personalized wake-up call every morning for a week.

32. Shine all his shoes.

33. Present him with a gift certificate good for "a day of errands," run by you.

34. Make him a montage tape of his favorite songs.

35. Give him a carnation for his lapel.

36. Plant him a window box garden to brighten his days.

37. Have his tennis racquet restrung.

38. Buy him a set of satin sheets.

39. Bake him a loaf of bread and serve it in bed with some homemade preserves.

40. Throw him and his friends a "superbowl" party.

41. Share your favorite poems with him.

42. Let him read your high school diary.

43. Knit him a scarf.

44. Buy him some goldfish to keep him company when you're not around.

45. Serve him a hot toddy on a cold winter's night.

46. Arrange a surprise reunion with an old friend of his (male or female!)

47. Plan a surprise birthday party for him.

48. Organize his desk, closets and drawers (permission first, please).

49. Arrange a weekend for two at the seashore.

50. Make him a champagne brunch.

Fifty nice things to do for her

1. Pick her up at work on a rainy day.

2. Send her a box of Godiva chocolates.

3. Offer to paint her apartment.

4. Take her to the ballet.

5. Pick her a bunch of wildflowers.

6. Cook her a candlelight dinner.

7. Buy her a puppy.

8. Tell her she's beautiful (just out of the blue).

9. Send her a card every day for a week.

10. Give her a gift certificate for an afternoon of beauty treatments.

11. Take her antiquing.

12. Refinish her old furniture.

13. Give her two tickets for a concert of her favorite oldies group.

14. Send a basket of fruit and cheeses to her office.

15. Give her a gift certificate from her favorite catalogue.

16. Hand her your credit card for an afternoon, (if you dare).

17. Take her to an art opening... and buy her her favorite print.

18. Send her a singing telegram.

19. Buy her a gold trinket.(you can never go wrong with gold!)

20. Reserve a row boat and picnic grove...you bring the lunch.

21. Take her dancing 'til dawn.

22. Buy her a tiny bottle of very expensive French perfume.

23. Take her for a ride in a hansom cab (horse drawn, you know).

24. Send her a balloongram.

25. Have a fix it day in her apartment (you do all the work).

26. Take her for a moonlight walk on the beach.

27. Rent two bicycles (don't forget the wine & cheese).

28. Have an old ring of yours reset for her.

29. Give her a membership to a health spa.

30. Take her to a quaint country inn for the weekend.

31. Buy her tortoise shell combs for her hair.

32. Build her a snowman.

33. Invite her best friend to join you two for dinner.

34. Buy her a book of poetry.

35. Take her to a chic restaurant.

36. Buy her some pretty (and sexy) silk underwear.

37. Offer to drive her to visit her parents.

38. Leave the Sunday paper outside her door with a single red rose.

39. Teach her how to check her oil and change a tire.

40. Buy her two love birds in a pretty wicker cage.

41. Offer to water her plants, walk her dog, etc. so she can have a weekend away with her friends.

42. Send her a love letter.

43. Take her on a one day cruise.

44. Throw her a surprise party.

45. Sign her up for racquetball lessons at a local health club (or tennis, horseback riding, etc.)

46. Buy her antique lace sheets.

47. Enroll her in the cookie or book of the month club.

48. Buy her a flowering plant for her apartment.

49. Send her a candygram.

50. Enroll her in a self-defense course (and offer to be her victim for practice sessions).

A simple, upfront way of letting someone know you're attracted to them, without seeming desperate

It's a mistake to assume that telling someone you find them attractive puts you at a disadvantage. Obviously, if it's done in a desperate way — if you make it look like the act of a drowning person — then it will have a negative effect. But if you do it simply, directly, openly and honestly, it's almost impossible for it to be misinterpreted, and — even more important — for it to go unappreciated.

Have you ever given someone a simple, straightforward compliment, honestly felt and honestly expressed — like, "You know, I enjoy your company very much," or "I want to tell you that I find it very pleasant being with you," or "Being with you really makes me feel great." To someone who's unaccustomed to using such expressions and *expressing* such feelings, the idea probably seems outrageous. But there's nothing outrageous in the reaction of the person who receives the compliment. He or she feels only pleasure and satisfaction, and perhaps a small dose of guilt at being so smiled upon by good fortune.

Some people, thinking themselves unworthy of such a compliment, may experience a moment's doubt when they hear it. But if you haven't laid it on too heavily, if you've avoided gushing and oozing and have been careful to be honest, earnest and forthright, you will come across simply as someone who's in the habit of saying what you feel in the most direct way possible.

Think of how *you* would react if someone in whom you felt more than just a passing interest suddenly told you of their own special interest in you. Wouldn't it be a good experience? Wouldn't you be happy that they were able to express so easily what you were just beginning to form in your mind? Isn't it exciting to be in the company of someone who feels that way about you and is able to *tell* you?

John Blake, twenty-nine years old, single, and feeling rather lonely at the moment, was at a party in the home of an old army buddy of his. Shortly after he arrived he spotted someone who interested him. She seemed about his age, was slim and pretty — and most of all, seemed vibrantly alive. She was almost constantly occupied in conversation with different people. John kept looking at her, and he saw that she had noticed his obvious interest. She didn't appear to be returning it, though — at any rate, he wasn't getting any clear-cut signals from her. John was frozen with indecision. After all, he told himself, wasn't she surrounded by admirers? If she wanted him to make an overture, wouldn't she have sent him some unmistakable signal?

Marcia, for her part, was aware of John's attention from the beginning; but since all he did was look, she was afraid to conclude that it was definitely an interest in her. She *was* slightly nearsighted, and, she thought, it might very well be someone just in front of her, or just behind or beyond her, that he was looking at.

Finally, when John was about ready to give up and call it a night, there came the opportunity that he couldn't pass up, or he would never forgive himself. He was alone at one end of the room, and she was alone—for the moment—at the other. He got up and went over to Marcia, and said (hoping he didn't sound too nervous), "I've been watching you all evening and wondering when I'd get up the nerve to come over and talk to you." And Marcia, laughing, replied, "You know, I've spent most of the evening wondering if you've been looking at me or at someone else around here. If I had been certain it was me you were interested in, I'd have smiled or something—but I just couldn't be sure."

"It's really crazy, isn't it?" John went on. "Here we've both been circling around each other like this, wasting most of the evening when we could have been spending it together." Marcia nodded. "Each of us was afraid to make the first move," she said. "I'm awfully glad you managed it, because I'm not sure I would have been able to." And John put the finishing touch to this beginning of their relationship (which, by the way, is still going on), by saying "You know, we've just been very honest with each other. We've told each other that we were drawn to each other before we met, were both scared, and were trying to find a way to connect. And we did it by being honest and saying so. I don't think I've ever had the courage to do that before. My name's John, what's yours?" She told him—that, and much more.

Telling someone how you feel about them, directly

and honestly, won't make you seem weak or desperate. Far from it! On the contrary, it will impress other people with your boldness, imagination, earnestness and candor. Who could possibly suspect someone of weakness who speaks so simply and frankly of what he or she feels? They can only admire and envy you ... and want to get to know you. It's the people who are afraid— of rejection, of "losing face," of letting anyone see their true feeling—and who let their fear keep them from doing the things they want to do—who are the weak ones.

So the next time you see someone who attracts you—walk over and tell them so. You won't be sorry.

Eleven very original, mostly inexpensive, fun dates to impress someone special

You've finally met the girl (or guy) you've been dreaming about. She's bright, sensitive, warm, pretty, and above all, fun to be with. The weekend is quickly approaching and you want to plan something really special for her. But what? Anybody can take her to a movie, and she's probably been to every restaurant in town. And bowling . . . come on, it's the 1980's.

Don't bother racking your brain! Instead read through the list of date suggestions below and see which one suits your fancy. Don't feel that you have to follow my itinerary exactly . . . substitute a few ideas of your own. If she (or he) is really exceptional, you might want to try out the whole list! Since there are a few things I suggest that you both have probably never done before, the excitement, thrill (and sometimes adventure) of the experience will add a certain dimension to the date . . . a pleasant oneness between you that you'll never forget. And while a few of these suggestions may seem a little odd to you, chances are your date will find them wonderfully creative and inventive. At worst you'll both have a good laugh, and you'll get an "A" for effort.

1. **The Spiritual Date:** This date, like most of the others, requires a little advance preparation. A few days before the evening of your date, glance through the yellow pages under the heading "spiritual advisors." Select the name of a fortune teller, palm or tarot card reader in your area. Make an appointment for two. Also take the time to stop in a toy store to purchase a ouji board. On the night of your date, begin the evening with dinner at a small, dark ethnic restaurant of your choice (a Rumanian one would be ideal, but they're tough to find!) From there, continue onward to you "spiritual advisor" to see what the future has in store. If you've never had your fortune told or your cards read before, you're in for a really wild experience. Once you've gotten into that mystical mood, finish out the evening back at your apartment over the ouji board. Remember, you're allowed to ask ouji *anything* you want!

2. **The Ivy League Date:** The setting for this date is a quaint college town, hopefully within an hour's drive of your home. If you or your date's alma mater isn't too far, or you don't mind a long drive, set out for "college town" in the early evening of a weekend night. When you get to town, ask a few students to recommend a local eatery. (Don't expect anything too fancy). After you've had a bite to eat, head for the college. If you've picked a nice night and a picturesque campus, you will enjoy taking a long walk. When you've had enough exercise, look for the student union and check out the night's activities. You're sure to find a lecture, concert, poetry reading, or exhibit to attend.

If you really want to end the evening authentically, hit the campus pub for a few frosty mugs of beer.

3. **The Disco Date:** If you've never gone club-hopping or dancing into the wee hours of the morning, this can be a terrific date. Perhaps the reason you've never boogied all night is because you don't feel comfortable out there on the dance floor. Fear no more, because by the end of this date you and your partner will be scuffing like pros! About two weeks in advance, make an appointment for a private lesson for two with a reputable dance studio in your area. Tell your date to dress up so you can leave right from the studio and practice what you've learned. In most cases, your instructor can suggest the hottest spots in town. After you've closed the clubs, it's back to your apartment for some intimate foot massaging (a dancer's dream!).

4. **The Chic Date:** A classy evening is what's in store for you and your date tonight. If you live near a large city, there's probably an ultra chic and incredibly expensive hotel which your date would love to visit. And the evening **need not** be as expensive as you think. Dress up smartly so that you blend with the crowd. Sit in the lobby and people watch (great fun if you enjoy personality picking). Most large hotels also have all sorts of curiosity shops on the premises. Browse through the shops and share a good laugh at the outrageous prices! If you skip dinner and just order cocktails at the lounge, the tab won't leave you broke (Although you'll probably pay $3.00 - $4.00 a drink). If you're lucky, the hotel you've chosen will have a piano player or band to set a romantic atmosphere. Don't be too tempted to stay over however; an

average room at a fancy hotel can start at $100

5. **The Winter Date:** If you live in a state where it snows, "The Winter Date" is a terrific way to spend a weekend day together. Get an early start, dress warmly, and head out to a country inn or ski lodge. Rent a sled or toboggan, and enjoy the brisk weather and perky atmosphere. Later, warm up by the fireplace inside the lodge (a must for this date) with a few hot toddys or perhaps some home made apple pie and freshed brewed cinnamon tea. Once you've regained your energy, it's back outdoors for an hour or two of ice skating. Your date will be so exhausted from the days activities, that she (he) will welcome a quiet evening for two cuddled up on your couch. On the way home, be sure to stop off for some deli sandwiches, and a light bottle of wine.

6. **The Dinner Date:** If you've finally met the person truly worth impressing, this date may be just the thing for you. Check a large newspaper under "Personal Services," for a chef that will come to your home for the night. Try to find one who will also serve dinner. (In my hometown, an Oriental woman will prepare a dinner for two, serve it in traditional style, dressed in a Kimono, and clean up, all for under $60.00). If you draw a blank, call up a cooking school for a recommendation. Discuss the menu with the chef beforehand and splurge for something very special. (This isn't an everyday date, after all). French food would be superb if your chef knows his cuisine (very romantic, you know). In most cases, he or she will bring the entire feast with him, so just have some good wine and appertifs on hand. Don't forget a pretty lace tablecloth, candles and good china. (Borrow if you must). The

only problem with this date is what do you do for a topper?

7. **The Date to Nowhere:** If you've asked someone out who you don't know well, a "date to nowhere" can help the two of you become very well acquainted. The trick to this date is not where you're going, but how you'll get there. In fact, getting there *is* the date. And I suggest a train. A few days before you're to meet, purchase two round trip train tickets to a destination a few hours from home. If there's a city or town you've been wanting to visit, now is your opportunity. Make sure the train has a dining car and bar if possible. You'll be pleasantly surprised at how relaxing and peaceful a train ride can be, especially with good company. Your train may not be the Orient Express, but there is a certain mystique associated with a long coach ride. So sit back, get into some revealing conversation and forget about time and reality. Who knows, you just may end up in Istanbul!

8. **The Self Improvement Date:** This particular date is most successful and most fulfilling when the two of you share a common and passionate interest. So I advise that you try this only after you've taken the person out a few times and gotten to know each other. Let's assume you've discovered that you both have a passion for old Chinese art. Begin your date by visiting a museum and strolling through the "Pottery of the Hing Dynasty" exhibit. From there, make the rounds of book stores and art shops, browsing leisurely. If you've got a little cash to spare surprise your date by buying her (or him) a small Chinese print or art object from the period. Exploring your newest discoveries over a bottle of wine at an outdoor cafe would be a

very nice way to end an already perfect day.

9. **The Farm Date:** Remember when you were a kid and your parents took you to your uncle's orchard to pick all the apples you wanted? What a good old time that was! As far as I'm concerned, it's still a good time and a *great* date. Do a little investigating; find out where the nearest orchard is, or where there's a farm that lets you pick your own in-season fruit or vegetables. (These usually charge by the bushel or basket). If apples aren't grown in your region, how about strawberries or blueberries? Bring along a pair of garden gloves and wear old clothes and worn out sneakers. After you've gathered all the fruit you feel like picking, tour the countryside and stop for lunch. "Sounds good so far, but what am I supposed to do with all the fruit?" you ask. I suggest having a bake off at one of your apartments. Look for recipes in a popular cookbook and shop for whatever ingredients you need. Whip up some tarts, pies, breads, and fancy fruit drinks. When your baking is done, pay a surprise visit to a few of her friends and let them sample your work.

10. **The Folk Art Date:** When I mentioned earlier that some of these dates were a little "weird," I had this one in particular in mind. Believe it or not, I suggest that you and your date spend an hour or two in a cemetery. Don't get alarmed, you won't be digging up bodies! What you will be doing, is making gravestone rubbings . . . a very popular folk art craft and a simple way to make an interesting hanging for your apartment wall. All you need to bring along is some white shelf paper (rice paper is even better) a few black crayons, and some masking tape. Try to select an

ancient cemetery, since old headstones are much more intricate and "artsy." Simply place the paper over the stone, apply some tape to hold it in place, and rub your crayon evenly over the surface until you can read it (It's always good to check with the cemetery first for permission). When you've completed your project, look for a park or rest area and have a picnic lunch, (which you've prepared that morning). On the way home, stop at a do it yourself framing shop, and get your rubbings ready for hanging. Help each other choose the best spot for your masterpieces in your respective apartments. You can be sure that your date will always remember that day since he or she will have a curious souvenir to hang on the wall . . . a **real** show stopper!

11. **The Exercise Date:** Here's one I'm particularly fond of since I've done it myself many times. It's such a great date because it's so unthreatening, yet it does a great deal to bring two people together. Simply, suggest an evening or afternoon of exercise. Now, tennis, racquetball, hiking, etc. are fine . . . they certainly qualify as exercise dates. But my personal favorite is yoga class. There isn't a city or town in the country that doesn't offer a coed yoga class these days and they're always inexpensive—$2.00 - $5.00 for an hour class. You put on some loose clothing and are then guided through stretching and meditation exercises. After the hour you'll both feel you've gotten a good workout, yet you're refreshed and ready for more activities. Another nice part of this date is that most yoga centers have saunas (almost always coed) which you're encouraged to take after class. This will put you both in a warm, wonderful mood and always seems to encourage intimate conversation. (Note:

When you're at your yoga center, ask about massage classes. Everyone's taking these today and it's a great skill to learn. Giving a massage is like giving a gift to someone. These courses are reasonably priced and they're great places to meet nice people. A massage class is also a great date and helps tremendously in diffusing any sexual tensions you both might be feeling!)

How to bring out the witty, charming side of your personality when you feel yourself starting to clam up

Remember the old saying about nice guys finishing last? It's true—they often do, at least in this life. So don't place too much emphasis on formality, gentility and manners. Here are some easy ways to keep yourself from "clamming up" and getting formal at social gatherings and when you meet new people.

A character in an old play, talking about her sister and the sister's husband, says, "She used to think he was the wisest, boldest, wittiest, most charming, etc., etc., of men. Then she found out he was only the nicest." There's the whole thing in a nutshell. It may be nice to be nice, but it isn't enough. What's more, it can sometimes actually stand in the way to be too nice.

It's hard to be witty, provocative, exciting and interesting if you're very concerned about doing the "right" things in some formal, Emily-Post sense. If your parents brought you up feeling that formal "manners" were very important, then you may have to put forth a conscious effort to overcome that. The stiffness that results from an excessive concern with etiquette—use of the proper forms of address, getting the last name as well as the first name and then not speaking up unless you know the name, waiting your turn in a conversation, being excessively deferential, and so on—all of these things have a deadening effect and are a deadly weight to carry around.

Don't worry about titles! Anyone who insists on being called by his or her title probably isn't worth your getting to know anyway. Try to remember first names—and if you don't catch the name, carry on without it until an opportunity to learn the name comes up. And make a contribution to the conversation (if it doesn't come naturally, then **force** yourself—the more you do it, the sooner you'll find it does come naturally) at any and every chance. Don't waste time waiting for the **perfect** opportunity. Don't pass up that perfect opportunity when it comes along, of course—but in the meantime, less than perfect chances to become a part of things can't be allowed to go by. And remember, you don't have to defer to people—with or without credentials—just because they may **seem** to know what they're talking about and because you don't know anything about the subject. This can really make you freeze up if you let it. Listen carefully; look for soft spots in their point of view; wade right in with a "But if you say ... then how...?" It will show that you listen well, think clearly and know how to formulate intelligent questions. And don't ever be embarrassed to ask for an explanation of something. There's no shame in admitting that you're not well-informed on a particular topic — no one can be expected to know everything. That's far better than standing there like a dummy, afraid to open your mouth for fear of putting your foot in it.

If you should feel yourself clamming up, go and get another drink. Incidentally, it's very important to start out by doing whatever is necessary to relax you, so that you will open up (but not fall apart). If one drink will do that, be sure to have that drink. If you know it takes one and a half, get that extra half drink under your belt. If it takes deep breathing exercises before you leave home (or in the elevator on the way up to the party), do them. Whatever! And then remember that the person you're talking to wants to enjoy him or herself as much as you want to enjoy yourself, and that both of you will be happier if the other person is having an obviously good and relaxed time. Try thinking of your companion as a friend, your best buddy, rather than as someone you want to impress. Convince yourself that he or she **wants** to enjoy your company, thinks of you as an equal and expects to be treated like one. If you can get yourself to really feel this relaxed friendliness, stiffness and formality will be impossible.

Another thing you can do when you feel yourself going overly formal is to think "silly." There's nothing wrong with a little giggling among friends. Begin to look for the funny things about your situation, about yourself, about your surroundings, the movie you've just seen, the guy standing at the bar, anything at all. And if you can't come up with anything real, invent! Punning is a much scorned but excellent and relaxing form of silliness. It's a surefire groan-evoker, but these are groans of **shared** silliness, groans that say, "That was terrible, but I get it, and I wish I had thought of it."

A guy I know, Karl, uses punning all the time as a means of relaxing himself and others and opening up a social situation that threatens to freeze over. "I found out at some point in my life," he said, "that all that business about puns being the lowest form of comedy is nonsense. All the groaning, at first, put me off. But then I realized that people were groaning to signify that they'd understood the pun, and then they'd continue to groan to cover up the fact that they were feverishly trying to come up with a pun of their own to top mine with. I remember what happened one evening when a pun I made started a chain of them that involved everybody and continued for half the evening. Somebody dropped a litter on the floor. I put my foot down hard on it. She said not to do that. I said that I'd just stamped it for her. Groans! Then somebody else said, 'Don't pick up that letter or it won't be stationery any more.' More groans! And so it went. Now I have the reputation of being the funniest guy around, and everybody is always relaxed when they're with me — and I can't help but be relaxed myself."

So remember that formality and stiffness (whatever you may have learned in your childhood) work against spontaneity and liveliness. Cultivate the warm, open, even silly side that we all have to our personalities. And above all, don't **worry** about looking silly. Worrying about relaxing too much is the surest way to keep yourself from relaxing at all. And the guy or the girl you're with — the one you want to get to know better — is going to appreciate the fact that you're someone who can be serious when seriousness is required and funny and relaxed when it's appropriate to be.

Force yourself to go out (And 75 more ways to meet new people)

At the hectic pace that most of us move at each day, it's no wonder we often find ourselves completely pooped when the sun goes down. While it's hard enough to muster up the energy to prepare a dinner or do the laundry, the thought of physically leaving our apartment for a night on the town can be totally devastating. So, too much of the time, we don't go out at all. We cuddle up on the couch, or settle into the bathtub, and feel sorry for ourselves for being so lonely.

Well, if you are really serious about meeting people, you've got to change. You can bet your bottom dollar that no one is going to waltz through your front door and settle into your lap. To meet new people, **you** have to go out and get **them**.

As tough as it already is to get motivated, it can be even harder when we think about getting ourselves physically together and heading out the door to the local "singles bar." We all know the feeling of too many nights in loud, crowded, smoke-filled bars, and the frustration of not meeting anyone who turns us on. But who says a singles bar is the best place for meeting people? Not me! There are dozens and dozens of other ways to make friends, have fun, and come away with a phone number or two.

At the end of this chapter you will find some of my suggestions for meeting new people in "unexpected" places. Use these as a start, but by all means add some of your own. Be creative! There are really very few situations in life that do not offer the opportunity to make a new acquaintance, or meet a new lover, so always be on the lookout. And remember if you choose activities that really interest you, as well as offer the opportunity to meet new people, you will not only want to get up and go at night, but you will look forward to it all day long!

A good way to start is by making a resolution right now. Promise yourself that whenever possible you will **FORCE** yourself to get out. You must circulate, circulate and circulate some more. People must see you to be attracted to you. And, believe me, if you're out there, people *will* be attracted to you.

One note: If you think you have an inordinate problem in the energy department (frequent listessness, fatigue, etc.) you might want to consult a physician. Or you might just be neglecting yourself, and in need of a new lifestyle to pep yourself up. Try putting yourself on a new health regimen which includes eating right, exercising, taking vitamins, and getting eight hours of sleep a night. Before you know it, you'll be a human dynamo, ready to conquer the world at a moments notice.

Try not to let the little everyday pressures of life drag you down either. There is no better way to forget a problem at the office or an overdue bill, than to plunge yourself into the excitement of a new activity. It's astonishing just how quickly your problems will fade when you don't dwell on them, but concentrate on having fun. It's not always easy, but try, really try, to push yourself into new activities.

So turn off the tv set, put down the mystery novel, and get out and try some of the hints below. You're sure to meet someone special if you push yourself a bit. The nicest surprises occur when you least expect them, so go out there and make one come your way.

1. Take a bus ride to Atlantic City (Las Vegas, etc.) . . . hang out in the casinos.

2. Bring your lunch to a friend's company cafeteria. Have your friend point out the interesting prospects.

3. Go to a ski lodge (even if you don't ski) and mingle at the bar.

4. Go roller skating.

5. Organize a high school reunion (maybe an ex-great catch is available again.)

6. Attend all kinds of special exhibits from antique car collections to miniature doll furniture.

7. Take a class in wine tasting — or have a class of your own!

8. Hang out in a large mall during your lunch break. You'll be surprised how many people do the same!

9. Look in the newspapers for organized singles outings, hikes, ski retreats, etc. (My typist met her husband on a singles hike).

10. Go to lectures at nearby universities (there are lots of sexy college profs!)

11. If you smoke, join a Quit Smoking group . . . you'll make many sympathetic friends.

12. Join a bowling league.

13. Get a part-time night job in a place with lots of single people.

14. Hang out in an airport lounge — travelers love a friendly face to talk to.

15. Go to the zoo. Offer to share your animal feed or bread crumbs with someone.

16. Eat lunch at a hospital cafeteria (it sounds a little strange, but they'll serve anyone, and there's no better place to meet an eligible nurse or doctor!)

17. Sit down with an old address/phone book and check out what long lost friends are up to.

18. Join the neighborhood arts council.

19. Attend your town meetings.

20. Frequent your nearby "Y".

21. Use a local laundromat instead of the washers in your building.

22. Browse through the aisles at a record shop. Strike up a conversation about your favorite group.

23. Go on a fishing excursion. If you hate to fish, sit back, relax, and get some sun.

24. Go ice skating at a nearby rink, or better yet, explore the romance of a local pond on a wintry day.

25. Have everyone you know invite three people (both sexes) and rent a huge campsite in the mountains for a weekend.

26. Take a course where you'll meet people of the opposite sex: if you're a woman, business and finance are good bets; for a man, fine arts, English, cooking, modern dance.

27. Take tennis lessons and get out on the courts. Organize a tennis party for your fellow players.

28. Go to a big hotel for a weekend and participate in all the activities.

29. Go to museums and look at the art (both living and dead) and start a conversation with a fellow art lover.

30. Join a health club. Organize a swimming party. Better yet, a co-ed sauna and jacuzzi party.

31. Go to the theater and make use of intermissions. Offer someone an orange drink.

32. Join a community chorus.

33. Go social dancing, folk dancing, square dancing. Get people to join in on a learn-and-enjoy party.

34. Go on a cruise and party all night (not difficult on a cruise).

35. Learn a craft—batik, potting, silver-working, you name it. Get people together for banana splits after class.

36. Go to street fairs and circulate. Offer to share your french fries with someone.

37. Join a co-ed consciousness-raising or sensitivity group.

38. Join a group therapy group (T.A. people are especially friendly). Invite everyone to your house for a marathon therapy session—all night.

39. Go on an Encounter weekend.

40. Go to a library. Look over someone's shoulder and say, "You'll love it—should I tell you what happens at the end?" (Even if you didn't read it and haven't the faintest idea).

41. Join the local Democratic or Republican Club. Invite people over to Meet The Candidate.

42. Go to carnivals.

43. Get involved in church groups. Have a Benefit party for a charity or for the church.

44. Join the local dramatic society. Organize a cast party after the play.

45. Go to the ballet and comment to someone on Nureyev's leaps.

46. Attend poetry readings. Organize an all-night reading of some incredibly long poem, with everyone taking part.

47. Join your high school or college alumni association and attend all their parties.

48. Join a tenants' association and agitate.

49. Take your pet to obedience school and get to know other owners.

50. Go to the beach or a pool and splash somebody.

51. Go to the Opera and ask someone if Scotto has a cold.

52. Go on bike hikes and greet other riders. Invite them to a bike hike-picnic.

53. Go on nature walks. Get groups of friends to go with you and bring refreshments.

54. Go to flea markets. A very easy place to start conversations.

55. Become an antique hunter. Buy some antiques and hold an auction/party.

56. Go to the park. Ask someone if the other half of their bench is taken.

57. Take your dog for long walks and let it get acquainted with other dogs being walked.

58. Go to rock concerts and hang loose.

59. Attend football, baseball, etc. games. Have a game-and-supper party.

60. Go to outdoor jazz concerts and invite people over to your place for a late party.

61. Join a local pressure group and throw a fund-raising party.

62. Frequent outdoor terraces of cafes and don't be shy.

63. Work for UNICEF. Have a Christmas-card-sale-and party.

64. Go on a Mystery Bus Tour and bring a bottle of champagne and plenty of paper cups.

65. Join the local Historical Society. Have a Rehabilitate Benedict Arnold party.

66. Join friends of Animals. Have a Save the Whales or a Spay Your Cat party.

67. Go to arts and crafts fairs. Ask a likely-looking crafts-person to explain his/her craft to you.

68. Join the ethnic organization of your choice (it doesn't have to be your own!)

69. Invite a local author to your house to discuss her (or his) most recent book. Invite plenty of men and women to listen.

70. Stand on lines for tickets. Queues can be friendly.

71. Walk in the rain and offer to share your umbrella with people (or ask if you can share theirs).

72. Invite all your friends who don't have families nearby to a big Thanksgiving or Christmas dinner and tell them to bring their friends.

73. Organize a huge scavenger hunt.

74. Ask your landlord if you can use the lobby of your building for a wine and cheese party on a Saturday afternoon. Put signs in the elevators inviting everyone to come.

75. Don't turn down any invitations!

Hold a party and meet new people

Parties. No matter what the occasion, parties seem to offer more promise of meeting someone special than anywhere else you can go. You generally know at least someone there, and simply by virtue of having been invited and "pre-screened" by the host or hostess, the other guests accept you as a friend...or a potential friend anyway.

If, for some reason, you find that there are a shortage of parties in your life, you've got to take action to change that. And there's no better way to start than by planning a party of your own. I've always found that one good celebration leads to another. You'll be surprised how quickly the invitations will come pouring in after you've had **your** bash.

Throwing a good party is simply a matter of getting yourself organized and planning the evening well in advance. You can often do it for very little money by simply having people bring their own liquors and a small dish of their favorite food to share. While there are certain holidays which we all associate with parties, a get-together for no reason at all can be just as much fun. But you can refer to my reasons for holding a party later in this chapter, if theme parties are still your style.

Make it a rule to send out printed invitations no matter how informal the party. Even if you hand print them and run them off on the company Xerox machine, still do it. The reasons are simple. Firstly, it's easy for your guests to forget the date or confuse the time if you've only invited them verbally over the phone, or asked them while passing each other briefly on the street. But, more importantly, a written invitation assures that the people you invite will have a record of your name, address and phone number when it's time for them to have **their** party. And that's the whole point...to get invited to more parties!

Now, you may be thinking that you'd love to have a party but you simply don't know enough people. Nonsense. If you have just five friends who you can ask, you're ready to have a spectacular party. Simply ask these five friends to invite three or five or ten guests of their own. Be sure to give them three extra invitations or more if they want. And get a rough idea of whom your friends will be inviting so you can keep the male/female ratio relatively even. And think about asking people whom you might normally overlook. It's fine to invite a very casual acquaintance, like the girl you smile to in the elevator each day. Or the guy who works down the hall from you at the office. Everyone loves a party, and they'll love you for inviting them. And since they'll be bringing friends of their own, you'll be meeting a whole network of new friends.

Once you've mailed out your invitations and you know approximately how many people are coming, start planning specifics. While it's nice just to get a crowd together for drinking and dancing, your guests are certain to remember **you** and the **evening** if you have a few surprises in store. Think up any clever gimmicks you can...games, a sing-a-long, live entertainment...anything to loosen up the crowd and keep the guests mingling.

After your guests have arrived and the party is under way, don't get so engrossed with your role as host that you neglect your own good time. People **will** help themselves to the onion dip and the asparagus sticks and the potato chips if they see you're busy socializing, and the food is out there. In fact, they're likely to loosen up a whole lot faster if they see you're comfortable just walking around, without hawking over them or catering to their every need. And remember, **you** are the host. You can approach **anyone** you choose **because** you're the host. It's simply your constitutional right under the laws of good partying.

Now, here are thirteen party themes that will leave your guests talking about you for months:

1. To ward off the ghosts and goblins at Halloween, plan a "come-as-scary-as-you-can" costume party. Hire a hypnotist or magician who will do a short show and then mingle with the guests later on. (They are not as expensive as you think). Don't forget to dunk for apples and to have a pumpkin carving competition. Costume contests will get a laugh also.

2. To bet on the Superbowl invite all your jock friends. Write the numbers two through fifty on slips of paper and place them in a hat. Select a cashier to sell the tickets for $1.00 each. A guest may buy as many tickets as desired, but they must pick them out of the hat (no cheating allowed). At the end of the Superbowl, total the scores of both teams. The person holding the ticket that corresponds to that number wins all the loot. The menu: spicy chili and lots of cold beer.

Obviously, this can be done for any sporting event (boxing matches, tennis matches, baseball series, etc.) and are especially good in a "rah rah" college football town.

3. To celebrate the Fourth of July, have a red, white, and blue party. Serve strawberry daquiries with the usual snacks. For a great summer refresher, top vanilla ice cream with crushed blueberries. Don't forget to tell guests to dress in red, white and blue, too. As dusk approaches, organize car pools to the nearest park with a fireworks show.

4. To pay tribute to the Beatles, have a "come-as-you-were-in-the-60's" party. Play Beatle music all night (of course) and have a trivia contest on events of the decade. Grab a partner and dance the skate, grog, Phillie Dog, swim and jerk.

5. To give Cupid a chance to shoot his arrow, arrange a St. Valentines Day party. Send out heart shaped invitations, and serve little heart shaped cakes (available in bakeries). Play lots of romantic slow dance music and organize a game of spin the bottle. (Don't knock it until you've tried it - it's a riot the second time around).

6. A just get-crazy-and-unwind party...for no reason at all. Cancel the dance music this time and round up some comedy records instead. I suggest Robin Williams, Redd Foxx, Rodney Dangerfield, Bill Cosby, Steve Martin, and Cheech and Chong for starters. Don't worry about the menu too much at this party. An ample supply of drinks and the entertainment you've provided will keep the party going! If you can afford a live comedian, fantastic. If not, have everybody stand up to tell one joke of their own.

7. To commemorate a movie legend, plan a festival of old Humphrey Bogart classics. Most city libraries will lend you a projector as well as the films. If not, you can rent the movies from a film rental company... just check the yellow pages. A large white sheet placed on your wall will do fine for a screen. Borrow a popcorn popper, and you're all set!

8. To celebrate the coming of Christmas...invite your guests to a *formal* dinner party. Ask a few close friends to help you with the cooking, or have it catered (if you get a big holiday bonus check). Hire an organ player to lead the group in a Christmas Carol sing-a-long. Tell everyone to bring a small gift ($5.00 limit) and have a grab bag exchange or rent a Santa suit and hand them out yourself!

9. To welcome those long summer nights, plan an *evening* picnic indoors (who needs the ants anyway?). Seat your guests on the floor around checkered tablecloths. Serve hot dogs, hamburgers, salads and fruit. If you've got the kind of crowd for it, separate everyone into two teams and organize indoor games like charades, pass the orange, and steal the bacon. A friend on a quiet acoustic guitar sets the mood for later in the evening. Drag everyone out to sit under the moon at midnight.

10. To surprise a really special friend on his or her birthday, make it a night not to be forgotten. Invite some people from out of the past (an old teacher, coach, dancing instructor, camp counselor, etc.) and lots of new faces, too. Try hiring a fortune teller or psychic for a truly memorable evening. You can also pool funds from all your guests a week in advance to put towards one special gift. And don't forget the birthday cake.

11. For a nostalgic evening, and a howling good time, hold a *co-ed* pajama party. I recently received my first invitation to one of these parties, and with vivid memories of junior high school pillow fights dancing in my head, I happily accepted. Here's how the invitation read, by the way:

> Paul Siegel and Susan Rancine invite you to a pajama party (co-ed) on September 14, 1981 at the Mayflower Hotel, Suite 29B.
>
> Buffet dinner served promptly at 8:00.
> Dress: casual.
>
> After 11:00: Dress for men: Pajamas
>   Dress for women: Pajamas or nightgowns
>
> Plan to dance, eat, drink, and play all those innocent games that were so much fun when you were 15. Pillows with just the right amount of stuffing will be provided. Bring a sleeping bag and blanket.
>
>   RSVP

With some trepidation I packed my flannels that Saturday night and headed down to the hotel suite which my hosts had rented for the evening. There were about 50 men and women there (all over 30, I might add) and after some initial discomfort, we all settled into one of the most natural, warm, and fun-loving evenings of our lives.

You can, of course, hold your pajama party at your home, and if you're worried about feeding everyone, charge five dollars per person. But no matter how you arrange it, be sure to have a pajama party soon. It's a party idea that can't miss!

12. Hold a party with an "amateur night" theme. As the host or hostess, you'll also be the "master of ceremonies" (rent a black tux, for effect, even if you're a woman). Set up a small stage area in your living room. Assign a few people to be judges, and go to a local hobby shop to pick up some cheap trophies. If you like, call your local newspaper and tell them what you're up to. Most local papers are happy to send a photographer over to take some candid shots of the festivities. And what a blast when they run a photo of your winning contestants in the next edition!

13. A Charity Ball. If there's a charity in your town or city that you really believe in, there's no better way to do a community service and to have a rollicking good evening at the same time than to organize a Charity Ball. It's easier than you think because you'll probably get a lot of volunteers to help. You can rent out a local VFW hall (tax deductible) or other location, and invite a ton of people. Charge ten dollars per person with the understanding this is a donation for charity. You might be able to get some food or drink for free from a local restaurant, and if you're a good talker you can often convince local entertainers (band, singer, etc.) to donate an hour...It's good for their image and they'll usually get their picture in the paper. Also send invitations to local politicians and other local "heavies" who consider it their civic duty to show up at these affairs and who often bring chic guests along with them.

You don't necessarily have to require formal wear either. You can hold a charity ball with a country band, square-dancing, and overalls. Or you can get a rock band and have people come in casual dress.

● ● ● ● ●

These are just a few party ideas you can try. Maybe you've heard of others that turn you on more. Great... give them a try! Recently, a divorced woman friend of mine, who had been complaining about a dull social life for three years, decided (with persistent prodding from me) to have a party. Her husband was a scoundrel, but he did have the good taste to build a handsome pool in their backyard before he left her. So she decided the natural thing for her to do was to have a pool party.

She took an ad out in the local paper, invited any single men and women over 30, charged $10 as a precaution to keep out undesirables, and waited for the big night. Fifty-three people came. She served wine and cheese, and hors d' oeuvres that her friends had brought, and the party was a huge success. My friend met at least five very desirable men that night, men who she would see again (most recently, Carl took her to see Pavarotti at the opera). But best of all, she's been *invited* to five parties since. And that was only nine weeks ago. I haven't heard a complaint about a dull social life in months. And it's the best proof I know for you to have *your* party *this* weekend!

A simple way to trick yourself into being looser at parties

To many people, a large party, or just a medium-sized one, raises spectres of hard work and promises of small return. Lots of small talk, circulating, trips to the punch bowl, moments of dread in the corner of the sofa with no one to talk to. But realizing one simple fact can change all that, can transform social gatherings from a chore to a delight: everybody is there for the same reason you are — to meet people, to socialize, to be friendly and to be befriended. You can trick yourself into being looser and friendlier by realizing that you're all in the same boat together, all there to see and be seen, to talk and be talked to, that it's all a two-way street with everybody expecting to give and get, the same as you.

The idea that you are singled out for discomfort and a sense of being ill at ease is simply not true. Very few people are so naturally gregarious and outgoing that they can make a go of a party without putting forth any energy at all. No one is born with the *natural* ability to make small talk, to glide gracefully from group to group or individual to individual. Even the most gracious of aristocrats in the old world had to have the art of mixing taught to them. Be secure in the knowledge that there is no one who comes by this ability without effort.

Then, the effort that *you* have to expend on "mixing" successfully will not seem so enormous.

Here you'd do well to remember that practice makes perfect. One does not acquire a successful party-going manner by *not* going to parties. It is by going, talking, circulating, mixing, flirting, making overtures, managing situations—in short, by *doing*—that one becomes better at it and that doing it becomes easier and more natural.

Take the experience of Frank. "Partying was always a chore for me," he said, as we relaxed over drinks in his apartment with his new girlfriend Linda, a chic brunette. "I never felt at ease, I was always tense and uptight. So much so that I would just as soon stay at home as go to a party ... and in fact, I wound up staying home a lot of the time." He smiled and took Linda's hand. "Linda and I met at a party. Just imagine, if I had stayed home that particular night.... Well, when I did go, I used to just sit and watch people a lot. It was an easy way out. And little by little I began to realize that everyone was in the same position—having to work at making a go of it. Everybody had a party persona, a certain personality that they put on for the evening, their party personality. The personality that was smiling, sparkle-eyed, pleasant, assertive, open, outgoing, receptive, ready to laugh and to joke. Once having realized this, I knew that I could do that just as well as anyone else. So I made the rounds of parties and I made the rounds *at* parties. But I was careful not to look determined or grim. I just watched other people, relaxed and flowed with the whole thing. I sort of imagined that we were all on a cruise ship, that we had paid a lot of money and were there to forget all our problems and responsibilities and just enjoy ourselves. It worked wonderfully that first time and it's worked ever since. Of course, there are occasional times — everybody has them and everybody's entitled to them — when you feel down and the last thing you want to do is spend time with a group of strangers. It's legitimate to ignore an occasional invitation. But you know, with this new-found ability to relax at parties, I sometimes find they're actually therapeutic, they're good for me when I'm feeling low. They help me to get out of myself, and that's important. Even during that bad time right after Doris and I split, rather than sit at home and brood, I found that I **wanted** to go out and be with other people — not necessarily friends, just people, any people. I had succeeded so well in learning how to relax under those circumstances that I had actually begun to use parties for all kinds of purposes, well beyond what I originally set out to do."

By watching other people, by seeing that everyone was having to make the same effort he had to make, Frank learned to "trick" himself into loosening up. But there's no magic to the trick at all, no sleight-of-hand. It's something everybody can do. The next time you go to a social gathering, look at those other people on that cruise ship with you. They've all invested a lot in this evening — this evening filled with new people, new personalities, new opportunities — and they're all just as earnestly concentrating on that major concern as you are. Knowing you're not alone, that everyone shares your concerns and your anxieties and has to work just as hard as you do, gives a great sense of security. That's the key — that simple knowledge that you're all in the same boat, working for and toward the same thing: human contact, a few hours of relaxation and freedom from cares, a few laughs, new acquaintances and possibly a relationship that will be more lasting, the kind that Frank and Linda found.

So climb aboard the ship and put on your party personality. Be the *first* to ask someone to dance—even if it means you two will be alone on the dance floor. People will join you soon enough. Wear an unusual, attention-getting button of some sort—"Save the Barbary Ape"? "Trust in God—She Will Provide"; "This Country Needs Nixon and Agnew" (*that*'ll start conversations). Walk around and introduce yourself to everyone you don't know—tell them you're running for sheriff and ask for their vote. Say hello to everyone you *do* know. Bring a bottle of champagne and offer a toast to the Queen (it doesn't matter **what** Queen). Toast your host or hostess. Sit in the lotus position and demonstrate yoga. Ask a group of people to join you in a chorus of "Nearer my God To Thee." Above all, remember that you're all there for the same reason—and then relax and enjoy.

Meet scores of fascinating new people in places you'd least expect

You can't spend your whole life at parties and making the rounds of singles bars, right? If you can, you probably don't need this book. But most of us have to spend an awful lot of our time doing terribly ordinary things, like working ... shopping ... cooking ... eating ... doing the laundry ... getting from one place to another. Would it surprise you to learn that the places where you transact the everyday business of living are richer sources of interesting, worthwhile people than all the singles spots and parties in the country? If such a statement makes you raise an eyebrow, read on....

Some of the nicest, most attractive, most eligible people have never set foot inside a singles bar, and the only parties they go to are those given by their close friends. This doesn't mean that you should religiously avoid bars and all types of organized singles activities: they can be lots of fun, and many fine relationships begin at such places. It simply means that it's foolish to put all your eggs in the swinging-singles basket, and neglect the hundreds of other opportunities that you encounter every day without even being aware of it. Not everyone goes to bars—but everyone (unless they are fabulously rich and have a staff of servants to take care of their every need) shops for food. Generally, married women with small children shop during the day; but the evenings and Saturdays belong to the singles. Do you see an attractive man or woman agonizing over which brand of canned split pea soup to buy? Walk over and tell them why you like brand X. Or ask a likely-looking prospect if they know where the corned beef hash is. Someone on the check-out line strike your fancy? Strike up a conversation. There are thousands of possibilities: the price of meat, why don't they give green stamps any more, is that really the best brand of dog food and what kind of dog do they have, anyway.

Ever take your dirty clothes to the laundromat? So do lots of other nice people. There's nothing easier to make conversation about than the relative merits of All and Tide—and then you can always joke about how it sounds just like a commercial. Have you seen those crazy commercials where the guy walks over to the woman doing her wash and offers her $50 for a dirty shirt? Try it—you'll get a laugh, anyway, and who knows—maybe a date. "Faint heart ne'er won fair lady/ gentleman."

My friend Jan told me about an experience she had going to work on the subway one morning. The train got stopped between stations, as frequently happens. Jan, being slightly claustrophobic, always dreads such incidents, but this time it was particularly bad for her, because the train was crowded and to top it off, the lights went out. She found herself shaking violently and put her hand over her eyes, hoping she wasn't going to faint. A man standing next to her asked if she was all right. He was a psychologist, he said, and he happened to be doing research on phobias. Would she care to describe for him what things caused her anxiety—tunnels, elevators, cars, closets, basements, etc.? Could she do him a huge favor and tell him about some of her dreams? Well, Jan got so involved in talking about her dreams of being stuck in narrow passageways—and in the gentleman himself, who she could see in the dim light was nice-looking and who had a soothing voice— that she forgot to be frightened. By the time the train got to her station, they had exchanged names and addresses and phone numbers ... and Jan had decided that there were certain advantages to being stuck in a stalled subway.

There are interesting people everywhere: subways, buses, stores, offices, factories, hospitals, restaurants, laundromats, post offices, banks, libraries, movie and other theaters, art galleries, parks, adult school classes (there are bound to be lots of men in business and finance classes; plenty of women in ballet, cooking and fine arts classes), beaches and pools, outdoor street fairs, hotel lobbies, waiting on lines (for almost anything except dirty movies), craft exhibits, sitting at outdoor cafes, walking their dogs, clubs, Y's, zoos, political rallies, candidates' headquarters, music festivals, ethnic food festivals....

Need I say more?

Keep someone infatuated with you date after date after date

Okay. You've gone out with that interesting guy or girl you met last week at Jane's party. You had a great evening and he/she seemed to enjoy it too. But will there be a next time? And if there is, will there be a third time? This is too good to lose out on. Here's a foolproof way to keep that certain person wanting to see you again and again. And again.

The key is to keep the freshness of the relationship alive. Your first evening together was so exciting because you heard things about the other person that fascinated you—a job he had as a guide at Yellowstone, or trip she took rafting down the Amazon. Or family experiences that were different from yours. You have one sister and he has ten brothers. Whatever it was, their lives were unique and made the evening special . . . even a little **surprising.**

People who like to be themselves aren't afraid to do what comes naturally to them. And since none of us feels exactly the same way all the time, that means changes—surprises—in the way we look, speak, behave. Military folks know the value of surprise. Surprise the enemy, and you're halfway to victory.

Now, the person you're dating isn't exactly the enemy; but surprise is still an awfully valuable weapon in your arsenal. By surprise, I don't mean jumping naked out of a cake (though even that might have its uses) or springing out of a closet as though you were trying to cure someone's hiccups. What I'm getting at is this: be a little bit unpredictable. There's time enough to be predictable when you've been married twenty years (even then, an occasional surprise doesn't hurt—but that's another story). Right now, at the outset of what you hope will be a long and rewarding relationship, what's needed is a moderate dose of the unexpected.

Let me tell you what happened about two years ago, the first time I went out with Bianca. I had met her, of all places, in a post office. I was standing next to her, and, observing the addresses on the envelopes she was holding, I said, innocently, "Is that your handwriting?" "Yes," she said, just as innocently. "It's beautiful," I said. "Like calligraphy. Where did you learn to write like that?" (Of course, you can't use this approach with someone whose writing is like abstract art dashed off by a gorilla.) Anyway, we got into conversation, and I took her to dinner the next evening. I wasn't *too* surprised by the outfit she wore—a rather severely tailored suit with a prim white blouse—since she had been very conservatively dressed when I met her. And her conversation, though interesting, seemed to fit in with the image: intelligent, well-informed, but not unusual. Her opinions were just about in the middle of every issue; she didn't use any language that you wouldn't want your D.A.R. grandmother to hear. In general, she seemed the very picture of a well-brought-up young lady. I liked her, but I wasn't exactly on fire. At the end of the evening, I walked her to her door. "I'll call you," I said, not at all sure whether I would or not. I leaned over to give her a peck on the cheek, not wanting to shock her by anything more frankly sexual than that. The next thing I knew, that sweet, demure young thing was holding my face between her hands and was giving me the wildest kiss I had ever had in my life!

Surprise number one.

When I had a chance to catch my breath and recover a little bit of my aplomb, I made as if to follow her into her apartment, to avail myself of what seemed like a clear invitation. But she held me back — gently but firmly, as they say — with a delicate manicured hand on my chest, and shook her head. "Goodnight," she said. "See you again soon."

Surprise number two.

With a kiss like that, I thought, she must really like me. I called the next day and asked if she was free that evening. She turned me down.

Surprise number three.

However, she **was** free the next night, and we went to a play. Her appearance was completely different: slinky jumpsuit in a clingy material with (as far as I could tell) no underwear.

Surprise number four.

And so on. To make a long story short, Bianca kept me guessing. I never knew what she was going to do, or say, or be, next. And I kept coming back to find out. She wasn't afraid to be inconsistent. If she felt her opinion about something needed changing, she changed it. She let her feelings guide her. If one day she felt sexy and loving, and another day she didn't, she behaved accordingly. She never let my — or anyone's — expectations of her dictate what she did. She was her own woman — though there were times when she *felt* like being frail and dependent. She didn't have a rigid image of herself in her mind that she always had to conform to; nor did she conform to anyone's fixed image of her. **She** knew who she was; she liked herself; she was fully aware that she was a very special person indeed. And so was everyone else.

We all have moods. None of us is exactly the same person today that we were yesterday; nor will we be quite the same tomorrow. Each one of us is actually many people — busy professional, understanding friend, sex object, devoted lover, child, parent, brother or sister, leader, follower ... these are only a few of the personalities inside us. Don't be afraid to let yourself be whatever it is you feel at the moment (unless, of course, it's something totally counter-productive, such as feeling really rotten when you're out with someone you're very attracted to). Let your body flow with your feelings. if you feel incredibly sexy, wear a sexy outfit. If you haven't got one, buy one! Say what's on your mind. Do what comes naturally (as long as you won't get arrested for it). Be mercurial, mysterious, endlessly fascinating. Be what *you* want to be. And you'll keep that guy or that girl coming back for more.

Twenty-five ways to improve your appearance

It's 8:00 on a Friday night, and you're getting ready to attend the grand opening of a new downtown club. As you're dashing around your bedroom you catch a glimpse of yourself in front of your bathroom mirror and stare at you reflection. Do you like what you see?

If you're like most of us, you can probably find dozens of things wrong with your appearance. We all have our "good-looking" days . . . those days when everything about us seems to fall just right. But for some reason, we don't have them as often as we'd like. Very few people are *always* pleased with the way they look. And while we would all like to see the face of Brooke Shields or John Travolta staring back at us, it's simply not going to happen. Frankly, life would be very boring if we all had that "perfect" look.

But, I won't lie and tell you that looks don't mean anything. They do, especially when you're meeting people for the first time. But it definitely takes more than a "pretty face" to look *really* good. For instance, have you ever admired a person's looks and found yourself thinking "He's (She's) really so average looking . . . there's really nothing that special about him. But what a great impression he makes." That person has mastered the art of being good-looking. He or she has learned to create an aura of attractiveness. And it's an aura that you can create for yourself too. It's not even that difficult if you know a few basics.

Impression is the key word here. Even if your nose is a little large, your hair a bit thin, or your chin somewhat protruding, you too can look great! While we may not have control over these imperfections, we can still do something about them.

It all starts with being clean, neat, and well-groomed. Crispness, and that ability to look "put together" (even on casual occasions) is more important than having the eyes of Paul Newman or the hair of Farrah Fawcett. Have you ever noticed how appealing those squeaky-clean Ivory girls look? Yet they're never stunning, and there's never anything terribly glamorous about their appearances.

Try not to be too obsessed with beauty. We all have different tastes and discriminations and what you may consider your major flaw, may be just the slight imperfection that someone else finds irresistibly charming and attractive. A cleft in your chin, for instance, or a slightly askew eye that lends mystery to your face.

And starting today, forget your bathroom mirror and reach for a full length one instead. Take in the overall picture. Scrutinize your clothes to see if they do you justice, check your shoes to make sure they're clean, examine your hair to see if it's the right hairstyle for you.

One of the best investments you can make, in fact, is the $20 you pay to a stylist who will consult you on a good hairstyle. Hair which is out of shape, incorrectly styled, or too long and shaggy, can do irreparable damage to an otherwise winning image. Once you find a hair cut that's right for you, be sure to keep it in shape by going back for a trim every six weeks.

Many of the steps that we can take to improve the impression we make are incredibly basic and simple. So simple, in fact, that we may be overlooking the obvious! Check out the list of "Do's" below and you'll see what I mean:

1. Wash your hair as often as necessary. Follow up shampooing with a balsam or cream rinse (It makes for great shine!)

2. Ask a professional hair colorist if you might not look better as a blonde, redhead, etc. (for men, too).

3. Check to be sure that there are no holes, tears, or missing buttons on your clothes.

4. Make sure your clothes are clean.

5. Make sure your clothes are ironed.

6. Keep your complexion glowing by following a careful skin care program. (A doctor or beauty care specialist can recommend one for your type of skin).

7. Exercise to keep your body lean and in shape.

8. Polish your shoes and replace worn heels.

9. Make sure your nails are clean and well manicured.

10. Carefully select your outfit to suit the occasion.

11. Brush your teeth three times a day and use mouthwash. (A toothbrush at work is a good idea).

12. Use a balm on lips to prevent cracking and bleeding.

13. Check to make sure pants and skirt hems are even.

14. Always use a deodorant.

15. Splash on a light after shave or cologne.

16. Shave whenever necessary.

17. Check socks & stockings for holes and runs.

18. Carry yourself properly (shoulders erect, stomach in).

19. Make sure that there is no lint, dog or cat hairs on your clothes.

20. Moisturize your face to help prevent wrinkles and keep skin smooth.

21. Shower daily.

22. Check for neatness . . . shirt tucked in, belt buckle in place, all buttons done.

23. Check your clothes for stylishness and sexiness . . . If you're a woman read the latest fashion magazines and study the photographs for the styles that would best fit your personality. (And unbutton one more button to add a 10% sexier look). If you're a man classic clothes will always be in style. But check some men's fashion magazines for a look that will give your wardrobe a little more flair.

24. Every so often have delicate clothes or cotton shirts professionally dry cleaned.

25. Always take a last minute overall look in a full length mirror before going out to assure that "put together" look.

How and why you should get really personal with the people you meet

Getting personal. Being intimate. These are skills few people seem to have mastered. But, they're critical to successful relationships. And since we all crave closeness and intimacy, people who are able to be intimate, who are able to break through the walls of superficiality and get personal, invariably have more people to love and enjoy more genuine love in return.

My own theory is that intimacy between people, physical as well as emotional, is a natural expression of feeling we all know by instinct. We're born knowing how to cuddle, how to ask for touch, how to get attention. As we grow a little older we plop ourselves into Mommy's lap when we feel lonely or scared, and we never worry about the consequences. It feels good. It feels natural.

But as adults we *learn* coldness and distance. We learn that letting someone into our lives, letting them hold us and make love to us, letting them share feelings and sharing them back, can hurt sometimes. And when we get hurt a lot, we stop sharing, stop letting people into our lives...we stop being personal. We let superficiality take over and build an invisible shield of coolness and indifference that keeps people away. It was a lot more fun when we were little.

We're not children and we can't drop into a woman's lap or fall into a man's arms as easily as we used to. But since giving affection is natural, it should not be as hard to recapture the ease of intimacy as one might think. And once we "relearn" this skill, it becomes easier and easier to try it with everyone we meet. And intimacy, even upon first meeting someone, doesn't have to be dangerous or hurtful. For instance, have you ever known someone who touched your hand as she spoke to you, or captured you with a warm gaze and smile. Some people can do this without being conscious of it. The effect this behavior has on us is wonderful...not frightening. We feel nurtured, cared for...we feel the person likes us and is attracted to us. And nine times out of ten, even if this person isn't particularly attractive, we begin to like them.

Other people can draw us closer with conversation. Think about people you know, especially those you go to parties with. If you observe these people in action, you're sure to find that there's always one person who seems to be engaged in deep conversation all the time. No matter who this person chats with, the dialogue just naturally flows and people automatically gravitate to his (or her) side.

How does this person do it? How do they move a discussion from business talk to feeling talk, from the mundane to the intimate? They break down the barriers of superficiality by getting personal, that's how.

They've learned one of life's most important lessons—there's not a soul alive who would rather discuss the weather than his or her feelings, wishes, fantasies, fears or loves. While we often feign chilliness and disinterest, we crave the warmth of an intimate conversation **that gets us involved.**

Since high school I've been friends with Diane, a very sweet girl from my neighborhood who always had many friends. Because we hung around with the same crowd, we often were invited to the same parties. When we arrived at a party, we always walked off in separate directions, content to talk with new people and gossip with old friends. If nothing had developed by the end of the evening we would meet and share a cab home. If you had heard our cab ride conversations, you would have sworn we had just come from two different parties!

"Hey, Rich didn't change much," I would comment. "Still at the same job. Looks a little thinner. Nothing new really." "Nothing new!" she would say with surprise. "The poor guy's been through the mill the last six months. He and Eleanor got divorced last May after she found out he was having an affair. He's now dating a woman from Paris named Monique, and he's just installed a hot tub in his townhouse. He says it's changed his whole outlook on sex."

We'd continue down the list of everyone at the party while Diane filled me in on the lives and loves of the same people I had just spoken with! She never talked about them in a careless way...just in a **caring** way. While I had simply talked with the friends we knew, she had made them feel like she really **cared**, like she was there for them, like talking to her would make them feel better. And very often it did. Kind of like falling into Mom's lap again.

After that night, I tagged along with Diane at the next few parties and found out the secret to her success. The trick was all a matter of asking the right kinds of personal questions. It was incredible the way people responded to Diane's openness. The more personal she got, the more warmth she generated, the more warmth people responded with. I found myself feeling fortunate that I had such a caring, loving friend. And I learned a heck of a lot from Diane about intimacy.

<u>By asking intimate and personal questions, we are letting others know that we care about them.</u> As long as you don't have a reputation for being the town gossip, or a Rona Barrett disciple, people will appreciate your interest, provided you are willing to share parts of yourself too. Beware though. At first some people may seem put off by your candor. That's only because they've grown accustomed to the protective shield people wear, a shield they've created in response. Once they realize your interest in them is genuine, you'll see that shield come down quickly, happily. You'll be amazed at the equal show of attention and warmth you receive in return. Love breeds love.

Listed below you will find a three part series of questions and statements to help get you started. The "everyday talk" section lists conversation openers which are not personal. They do not get the person you're speaking with involved. This is the kind of chatter you should try and stay away from. However, if you find it really difficult to be personal at first, then by all means, use one of these lines. As conversation openers they're useful and they represent a step in the right direction.

The "more personal" selections are the kinds of questions that are not intensely personal but are a great improvement. They do get the person involved because they require an answer. You might want to consider them "warm-ups" to more personal talk.

Finally, there is the "personal" section. When you're able to use these questions comfortably and honestly, you can consider yourself a graduate of the "How To Get Personal" course. They're a little probing, so always say them with a warm, honest, reassuring smile. And then you'll be able to bask in the good feelings of being able to get intimate with anyone you meet.

Everyday Talk

1. What do you think of this weather?

2. Nice place here, isn't it?

3. Can you believe the cost of living has just gone up again?

4. I can't get over how much traffic there was tonight.

5. They sure make a strong drink here, don't they?

6. Did you see that country and western special on T.V. last night?

7. I just read this great novel called **Separate Vacations.**

8. Boy, those Yanks are really something.

9. Wow, did the I.R.S. stick it to me this year.

10. There are certainly some sharp dressers in the place.

More Personal

1. Do you come from a big family?

2. Where did you go to school?

3. Do you like living in New York?

4. What made you come here tonight?

5. What kind of work do you do?

6. Where did you take vacation this year?

7. What's your favorite kind of food?

8. Where do you usually hang out?

9. Do you play, tennis, racquetball, etc.?

10. What's your idea of a great night out?

Personal

1. Have you ever been involved with someone you really loved?

2. How do you know we won't have a great time together unless we try?

3. What do you wear to bed when you're sleeping alone?

4. Where's the most outrageous place you've ever made love?

5. What are you looking for in a man (woman)?

6. Do you consider yourself more of a physical or emotional lover?

7. Tell me the circumstances surrounding the loss of your virginity? (said with a smile)

8. How did you spend the most romantic evening of your life?

9. What's the most sensuous thing you've ever had **done** to you?

10. Have you ever had a broken heart? What did it take to mend it?

Learn how to project a healthy, natural sex appeal

That gorgeous thing over there (who looks just like Robert Redford or Raquel Welch) doesn't have to do a thing to be sexy. When you look like that, all you have to do is look like that, and you've got it made. That's the way most people think and it's probably the way you think. But it isn't so. Even the "sex objects" have a certain amount of work to do. Granted, it's somewhat easier for them. But it's not all whipped cream.

Some pretty good-looking people have been quoted on some of the drawbacks of being very good-looking, they are automatically thought of as being all booked up. That is, they are intimidating. Everybody says, "oh, he or she is so good-looking that they'd never even talk to me. So why bother?" This puts the burden on the good-looking person of knowing how to project his or her interest and availability. Just *being* naturally sexy isn't even enough, you've got to get across the message that you're *interested*.

The key word here is "project": it's not enough to be or think sexy, you've got to project sexy. You can't be a slouch—you can never get away with being lazy. You've got to work at it.

Projecting healthy and natural sex appeal starts with feeling sexy. But it doesn't end there. It involves letting people know (at least, those people you *want* to get the message) that you feel loving, warm and passionate, that you enjoy personal involvements and attachments, that you think the human body is beautiful and that you like to touch and be touched, to kiss and caress.

How to do all this? First off, develop a manner that shows a relaxed naturalness where human contact is involved. When sitting down in a group, don't sit as far away from everyone as possible and avoid any contact with anyone else. On the contrary, sit down right next to someone, not in a blatant way, as though in another minute your tongue's going to be hanging out, but naturally and easily without calling anyone's attention to it. When standing and talking to people, stand as close to them as you like, and don't back off as the conversation proceeds unless your far-sightedness is beginning to scramble your brain. And when standing or sitting with someone you find attractive, don't be afraid to touch, either casually and inadvertently—arm to arm or knee to knee—or directly and intentionally—reach out and take an arm, tap on a shoulder, take hold of two shoulders, give a hug if it can be called for, peck on the cheek at the slightest provocation—and develop a whole repertoire of your own personal langauge of body contact. The body speaks louder than words in saying, "I'm a sensual, sexual person." And if someone touches you, for heaven's sake don't jump or flinch—even if it's not someone you're attracted to. You never know who might be watching. And we're not talking about groping, remember, but about the kind of touching that isn't prurient but testifies to a healthy, natural sexuality.

The eyes play a tremendous role in the projection of sexuality. The way you look at someone is often a clear signal of what and how you're feeling about them and about sexuality in general. Don't stare blankly—and don't look everywhere else *but* at the person you're talking to. Both extremes are counterproductive, and you can come across as being either catatonic or shifty. Look over approvingly—but once again I underline *naturally*—all parts of the person from feet to hair. (Everyone is excited by obvious visual approval from someone else.) Hair is very sensual stuff: look at it as if you could feel it—or would like to. Look at a mouth as if you would like to taste it and feel it. Feast your eyes on hands as they gesticulate at you. And so forth. And let it be clearly understood that as much as you enjoy someone else, you also like to be enjoyed yourself. Let it be seen that you take pleasure in being looked at, that you're proud of yourself and of your body and you're pleased that someone else enjoys looking at you.

Verbally, too, don't be afraid to be communicative, to actually come out and say in so many words what you are trying to say with actions and eyes. Give compliments that show what you like. If you're dying to run your fingers through someone's hair, don't compliment them on their hairdo, but on the silkiness or glossiness or curliness or whatever of the hair. If a mouth is appealing, don't just say it's a nice mouth, say it's a sensual mouth, a generous, loving mouth, maybe even a delicious mouth. Get the *sensual* message across.

"I was always looking into corners or out of windows," my friend, Barry, a bachelor and an accountant, told me. "Only occasionally did I force myself to look into the eyes of the people I was speaking to. And as far as touching was concerned, forget it. That was something that theatrical types and Russians did, not me. But then I had an experience which was so outrageous, and at the same time so delightful, that I decided I would just have to change the way I was behaving. I met a woman at a party that some mutual friends of ours gave at their apartment. When she was introduced, she smiled broadly, shook my hand with both of hers, and then sat down next to me on the couch. It had the kind of cushions that you sink down—and she sat with her shoulder and her thigh right up against me—none of this 'polite distance' stuff—and immediately put a hand on my knee, and told me I had some lovely hairs on my earlobes, while she breathed on my cheek (I didn't even know I had hairs on my earlobes!). But she didn't hang on me. She went away and spent time with other people and then came back to me. I of course found myself pulled back to her again and again. And I noticed she was generally that same close physical way with just about everybody, and everybody seemed to like it, though she wasn't even especially good-looking—her mouth was too big and her eyes were too close together. It made me a little jealous of all those others. But she clearly enjoyed people and touching and being close, and besides being sexy, it was also kind of joyous. One of the times when we got back together, she hugged me, kissed me on the cheek and made a little noise of pleasure, and then said, quite casually, "How's it going? Having a good time?" She talked to me some more and then was off again. She obviously felt good about herself, and she made me feel good about her and about myself. I made it a point to see her again—and being with her always does that for me. Lovely hairs on my earlobes—can you imagine?"

Let yourself enjoy people openly and honestly, the

way they look, feel and smell; and, keeping clear in your mind the difference between looking lecherous and just letting your natural sexuality show itself proudly. Don't be afraid to let your feelings move you to an occasional almost outrageous gesture. Being timid and retiring will never get you anywhere; doing something a little startling, but nice, and flattering to someone else, will make them feel good—and there's nothing people like more than people who make them feel good.